A-Z PORTS

REFERENCE

Motorway	**M27**
A Road	A27
B Road	B3333
Dual Carriageway	
One-way Street Traffic flow on A Roads is also indicated by a heavy line on the driver's left.	
Road Under Construction Opening dates are correct at the time of publication	
Proposed Road	
Restricted Access	
Pedestrianized Road	
Track / Footpath	
Residential Walkway	
Railway	Tunnel / Station / Level Crossing
Built-up Area	STONE ST.
Local Authority Boundary	
National Park Boundary	
Post Town Boundary	
Postcode Boundary (within post town)	
Map Continuation	10 / Large Scale City Centre 4

Car Park (selected)	P
Church or Chapel	†
Cycleway (selected)	🚲
Fire Station	■
Hospital	H
House Numbers (A & B Roads only)	83 96
Information Centre	i
National Grid Reference	470
Park & Ride	Tipner P+R
Police Station	▲
Post Office	★
Safety Camera with Speed Limit Fixed Cameras and long term road works cameras. Symbols do not indicate camera direction.	30
Toilet: without facilities for the Disabled	▽
with facilities for the Disabled	▽
Disabled use only	▽
Viewpoint	✳ ✳
Educational Establishment	▢
Hospital or Healthcare Building	▢
Industrial Building	▢
Leisure or Recreational Facility	▢
Place of Interest	▢
Public Building	▢
Shopping Centre or Market	▢
Other Selected Buildings	▢

SCALE

Large Scale Pages 4-5	1:7,920		Map Pages 6-57	1:15,840
0	⅛	¼ Mile	0	¼	½ Mile
0	100	200	300	400 Metres	0	250	500	750 Metres
8 inches (20.32 cm) to 1 mile	12.63 cm to 1 km		4 inches (10.16 cm) to 1 mile	6.31 cm to 1 km

EDITION 8 2017
Copyright © Geographers' A-Z Map Co. Ltd.

© Crown copyright and database rights 2017 OS 100017302.

Safety camera information supplied by www.PocketGPSWorld.com.
Speed Camera Location Database Copyright 2017 © PocketGPSWorld.com

A-Z AZ AtoZ
registered trade marks of
Geographers' A-Z Map Company Ltd
www./az.co.uk

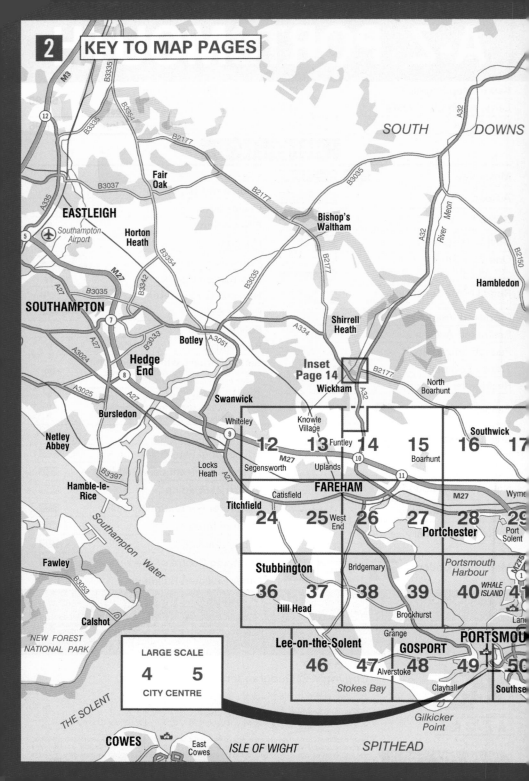

M3

B3335

12

B3335

B3354

B2177

Fair
Oak

B3037

SOUTH   DOWNS

B3035

A32

River Meon

B2150

EASTLEIGH

Southampton
Airport

5

Horton
Heath

B3354

Bishop's
Waltham

A32

Hambledon

M27

A27

B3035

B3342

B3035

B2177

SOUTHAMPTON

7

B3033

Botley

A3051

A334

Shirrell
Heath

North
Boarhunt

8

Hedge
End

A3024

A27

A3025

Inset
Page 14

B2177

Wickham

A32

Swanwick

Knowle
Village

Bursledon

Whiteley

9

12   13 Funtley 14   15   16   17

Netley
Abbey

Locks
Heath

M27

Segensworth Uplands

10

Boarhunt

Southwick

B3397

A27

Catisfield

FAREHAM

11

M27

Wyme

Hamble-le-
Rice

Titchfield

24   25 West
                End   26   27   28   29
                                          Portchester Port
                                                        Solent

Fawley

B3053

Stubbington

Bridgemary

Portsmouth
Harbour

M275

1

36   37   38   39   40 WHALE   41
                                            ISLAND

Calshot

Hill Head

Brockhurst

Lane

NEW FOREST
NATIONAL PARK

Lee-on-the-Solent

Grange

GOSPORT

PORTSMOU

LARGE SCALE

4   5

CITY CENTRE

46   47 Alverstoke 48   49   50

Stokes Bay

Clayhall

Southse

THE SOLENT

Gilkicker
Point

COWES   East
                Cowes   ISLE OF WIGHT   SPITHEAD

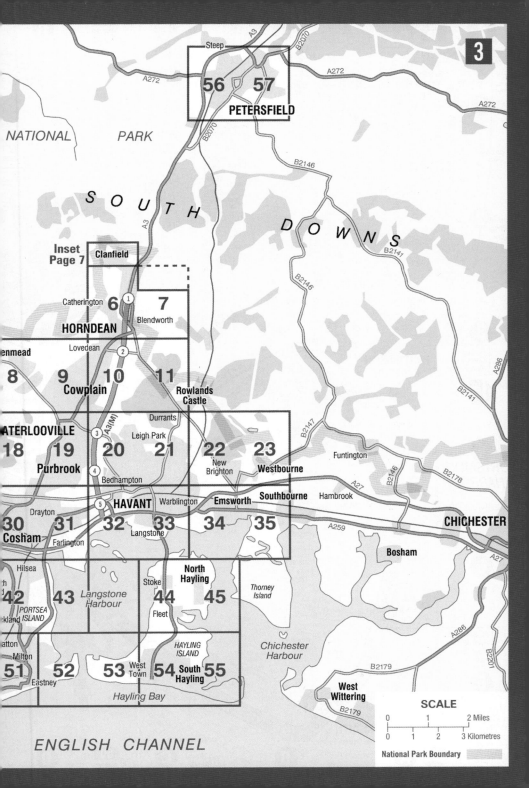

3

NATIONAL   PARK

S O U T H   D O W N S

A272
A3
B2070
A272
A272
A272
Steep
56   **57**
PETERSFIELD
B2070
B2146
B2141
B2146
B2146
A286

Inset Page 7
Clanfield
Catherington
6   ①   **7**
Blendworth
HORNDEAN
Lovedean
②
8   **9**   **10**   **11**
enmead
Cowplain
Rowlands Castle
A3
A3(M)
Durrants
③
Leigh Park
18   **19**   **20**   **21**   **22**   **23**
ATERLOOVILLE
Purbrook
New Brighton
Westbourne
④
Bedhampton
Funtington
B2147
B2146
B2178
A27
Hambrook
Southbourne
⑤
HAVANT   Warblington   **Emsworth**
30   **31**   **32**   **33**   **34**   **35**
Drayton
Cosham   Farlington   Langstone
A259
CHICHESTER
Hilsea
Bosham
42   **43**   **44**   **45**
Stoke
North Hayling
PORTSEA ISLAND
Langstone Harbour
Fleet
Thorney Island
A27
atton
Milton
HAYLING ISLAND
Chichester Harbour
51   **52**   **53**   **54**   **55**
Eastney
West Town
South Hayling
Hayling Bay
B2179
West Wittering
B2179
A286
B2201

ENGLISH CHANNEL

SCALE
0   1   2 Miles
0   1   2   3 Kilometres
National Park Boundary

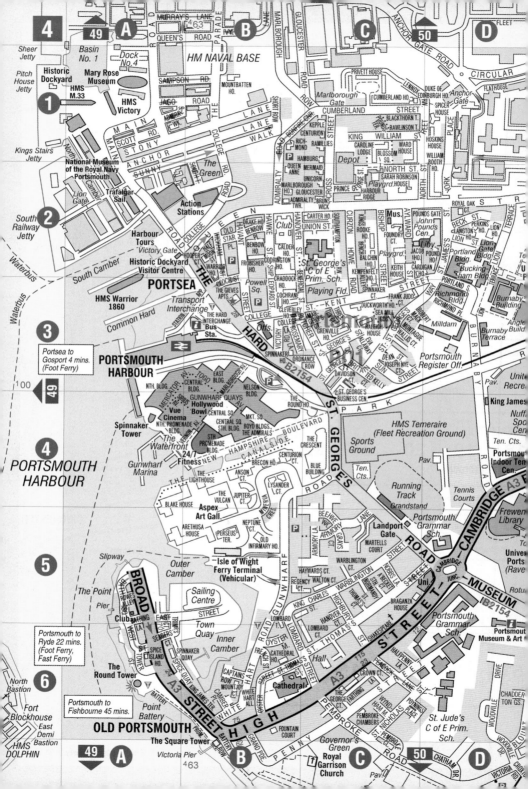

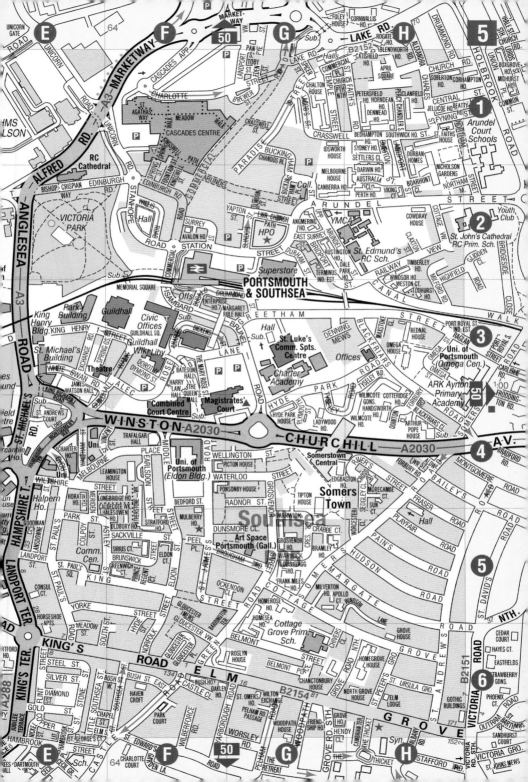

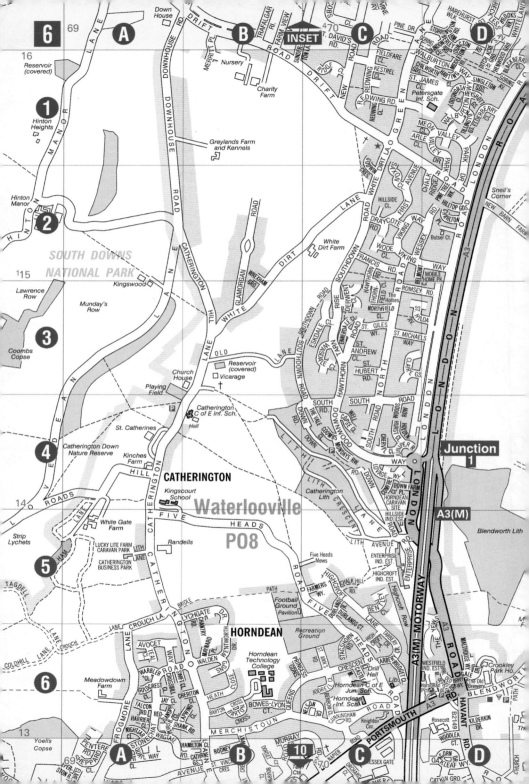

Sunnyfields

EAST

Clanfield
Chase

LITTLE HYDEN LA.

BRAMBLE CL.

Clanfield
Jun. Sch.

MEON LA.

NORTH

ORCHARD
CHURCH CL.

Swallow
Ct.

HOMEFIELD WY.

Manor
Farm

Downs
View

DOWNS ROAD

LANE

470

471

Petersfield

Recreation
Ground

Pav.

SOUTH DOWNS NATIONAL PARK

1

CLANFIELD

KINGSBURY CT.

WILLIS RD.

HAMBLEDON RD.

Hall

NICKLEBY RD.

POND LA.

**Waterlooville
PO8**

PEAK RD.

PIPERS

MEAD

SWORD CL.

Barnfield

Down
House

DOWNHOUSE RD.

DRIFT

MERRITT PL.

TRAFALGAR RD.

FARM VIEW

SOUTH

MANOR LA.

HINTON

ROAD

WINDMILL CL.

ROAD

ROSEWOOD GDS.

SANDAL WOOD CL.

ALDRIDGE CL.

JACOBS CL.

SUNDERTON ROAD

ST. DAVID'S RD.

BEECH

HAZEL

WHITE BEAM

HAZEL RISE

OAK RD.

HAWTHORNE

MAPLE RD.

SYCAMORE CL.

CRESCENT ROAD

GROVE

GREEN

PINE DR.

REDWING ROAD

STORRINGTON

GORING

MEADOWCROFT

ENDAL WAY

HAREHURST WLK.

DUNCTON RD.

REDNVIEW LA.

GREEN

DOWN WY.

APPLEY WY.

SNOWFLOWER

TEGLESE

GROVE

FOXGLOVE WY.

CLOVE DR.

BILBERRY

COLUMBINE

BEE ORCHD.

OAK LA.

DEWBERRY

WELLS

MARK

BECKLES AV.

BROOKS

WHITELAND

LONDON RD.

WAY

ON GDNS.

2

LONDON — A3 — RD.

116

HAWQUINS

New
Barn Farm

BARN

LANE

SOUTH

LANE

3

Netherley
Down

FARM

LANE

SOUTH DOWNS NATIONAL PARK

4

14

Crabden
Row

CRABDEN

DUCKSTILE

DUCKPOND LA.

Blendworth
Farm

Six Bells
Farm

Southview
Farm

Play
Fld.

HORNDEAN

ROAD

Broxburn
House

BOYES

LANE

LANE

Wick
Farm

5

BLENDWORTH

St. Giles
Farm

WICK HANGER

The New
Blendworth
Centre

Cadlington
House

LANE

WOODHOUSE LA.

Idsworth
House

Murrants

6

13

Hook
Cottage

Nobles
Farm

PATTERSONS

Idsworth
Villa

IDSWORTH PARK

73

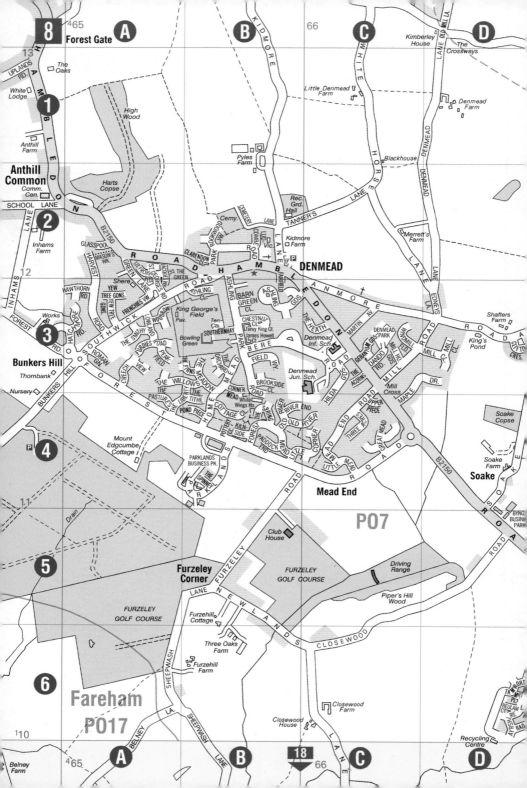

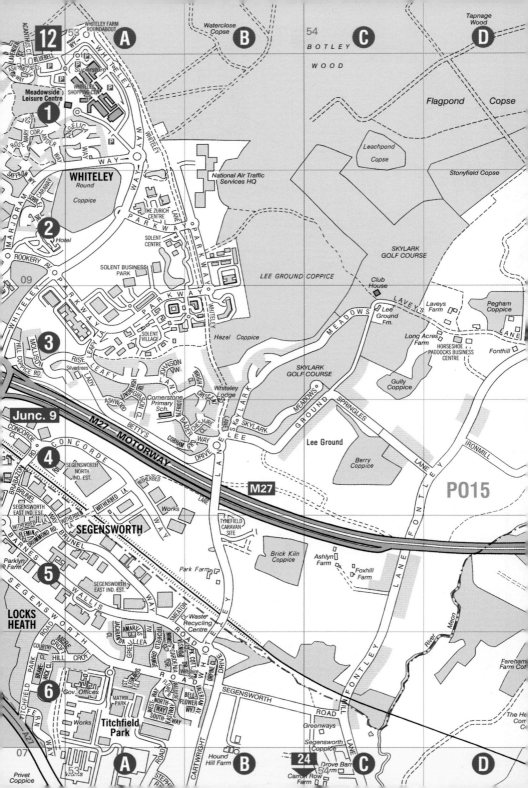

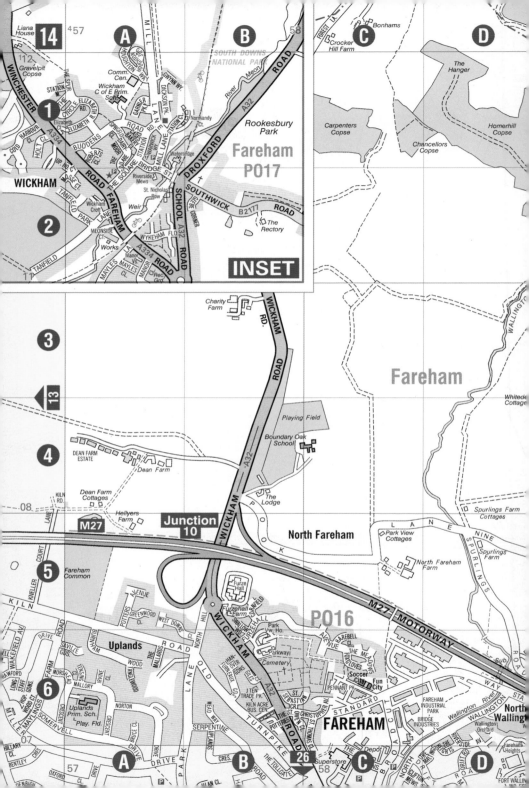

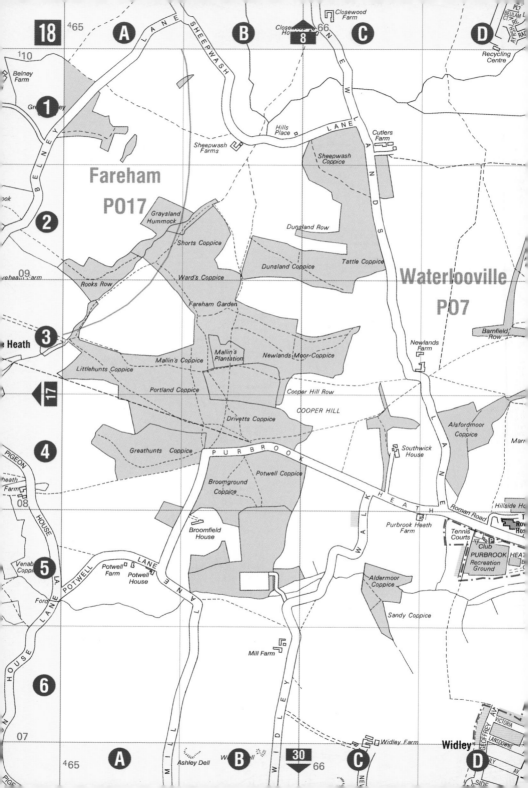

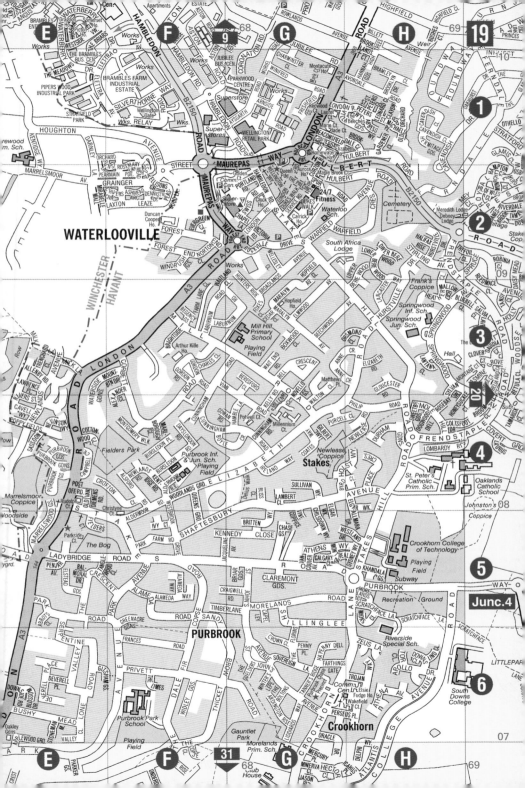

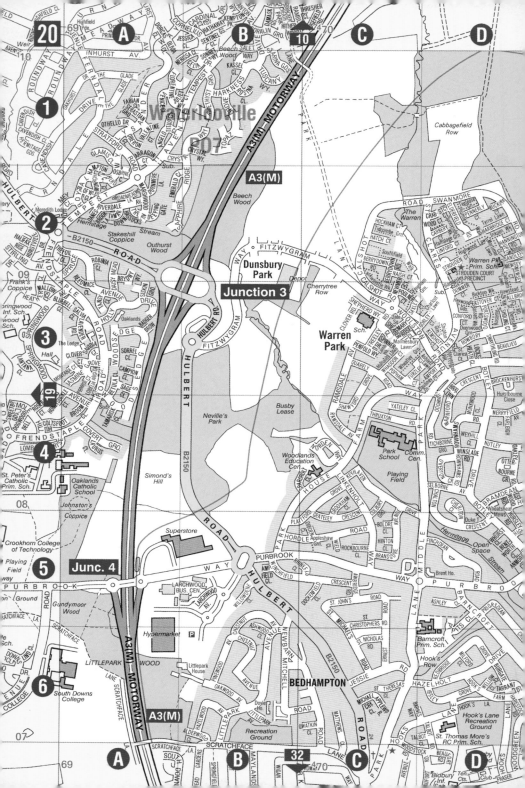

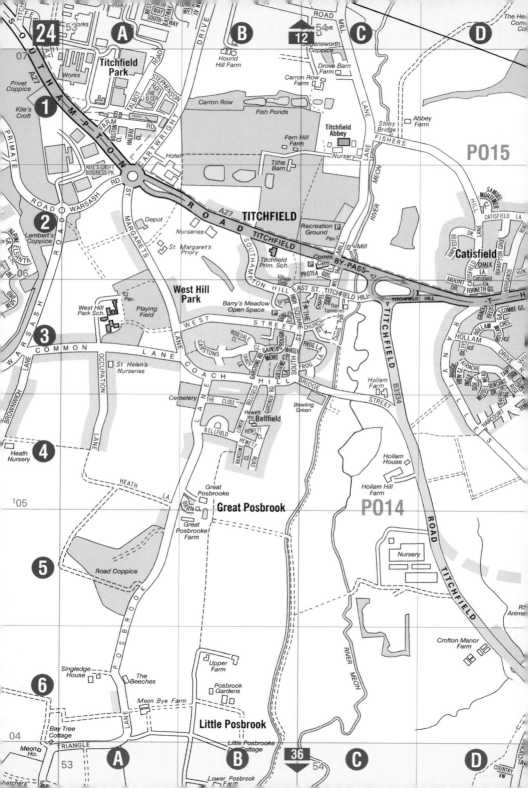

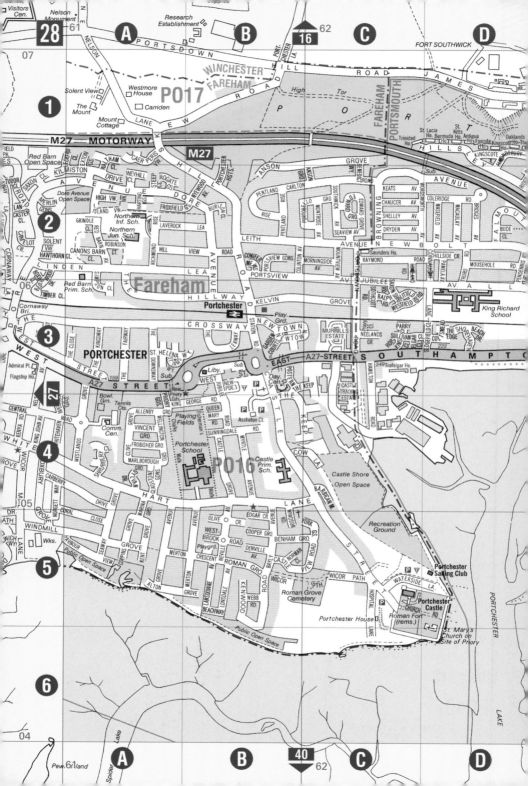

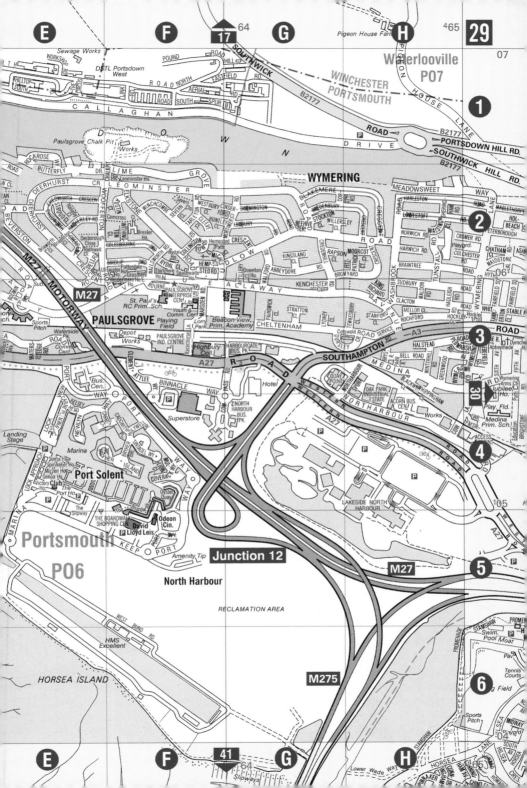

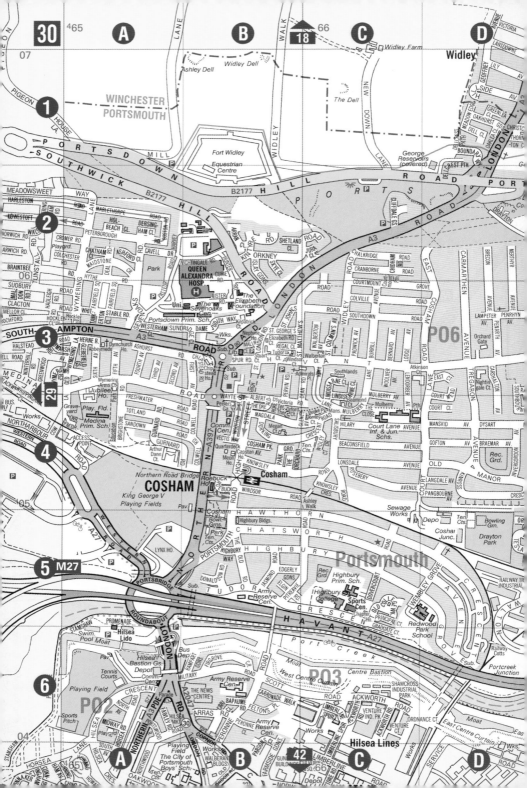

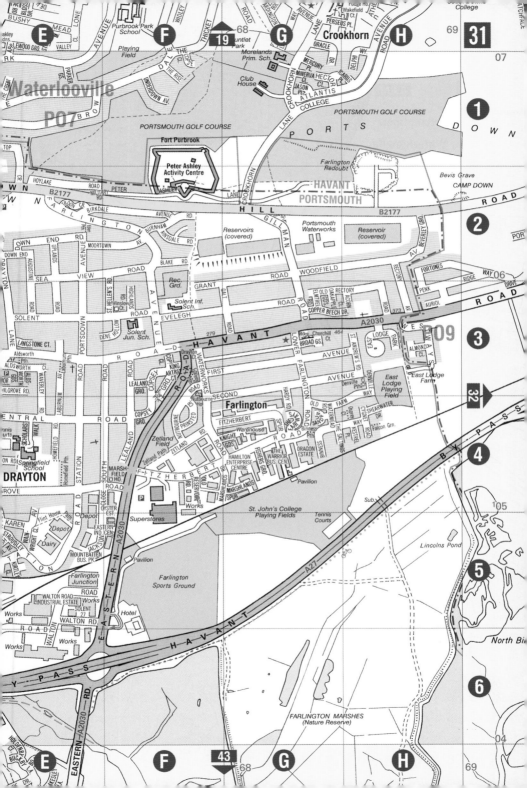

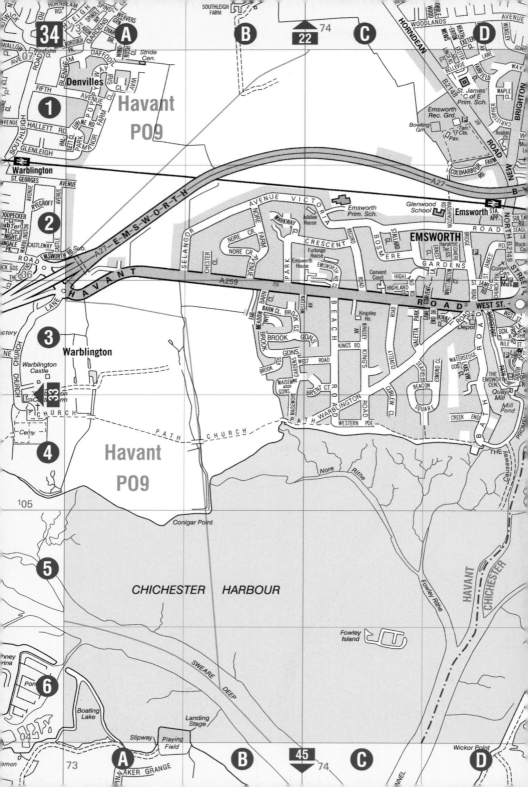

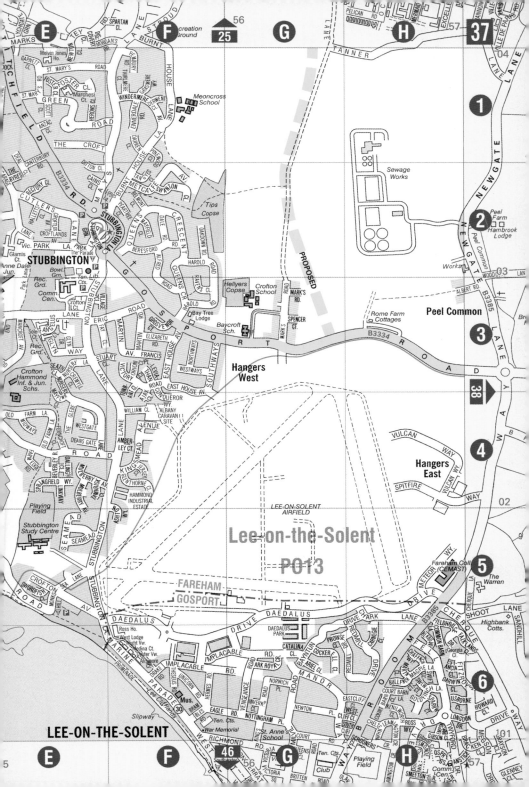

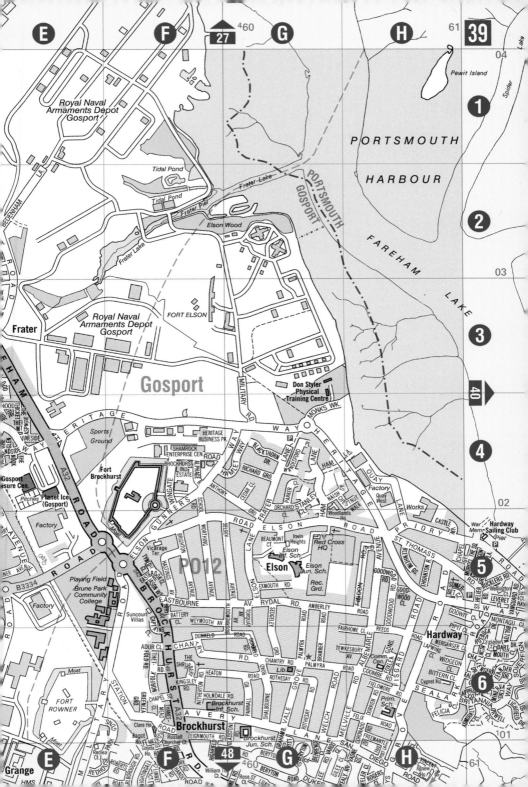

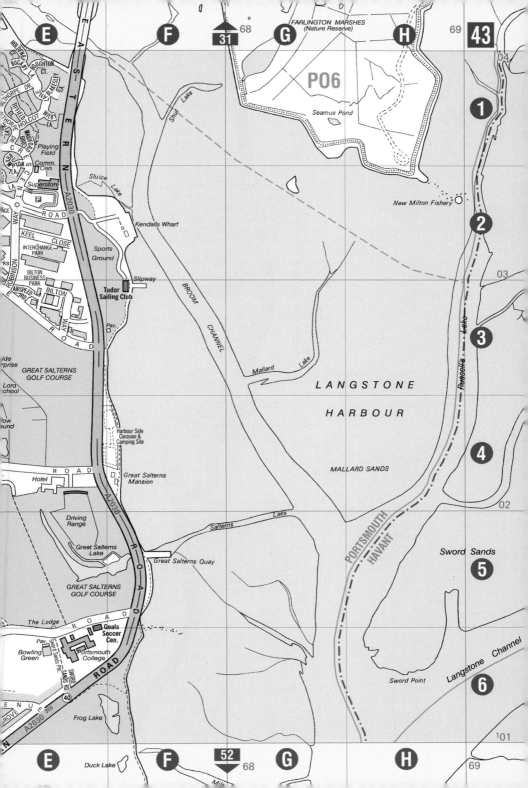

E   **F**   **31** 68   **G**   **H**   69   **43**

FARLINGTON MARSHES
(Nature Reserve)

PO6

Seamus Pond

1

04

HOLKHAM DR
BUCKLAND
BOUGHTON CT.
TITHFIELD
HOLCOT
WILB'N LA.
BLOMESLEY LA.
MADRESF D
THORP
CRESCENT
LA.

Playing
Field

Comm.
Cen.

Superstore

P

Sluice Lake

Shut Lake

New Milton Fishery

2

Kendalls Wharf

KEEL CLOSE

INTERCHANGE
PARK

Sports
Ground

03

BILTON
BUSINESS
PARK
AIRSPEED
ROBINSON
RD
BILTON
WAY

Slipway

Tudor
Sailing Club

Pav.

3

BROOM CHANNEL

Russells Lake

 side
erprise

GREAT SALTERNS
GOLF COURSE

Lord
chool

ow
und

Mallard Lake

L A N G S T O N E

H A R B O U R

4

Harbour Side
Caravan &
Camping Site

Great Salterns
Mansion

MALLARD SANDS

02

Hotel

ROAD

A2030

Driving
Range

Great Salterns
Lake

Salterns Lake

Great Salterns Quay

PORTSMOUTH
HAVANT

Sword Sands

5

GREAT SALTERNS
GOLF COURSE

The Lodge

Goals
Soccer Cen.

Bowling
Green

Pav.

Portsmouth
College

SWORD
SANDS RD
Sword Sands Pth.

R O A D

Sword Point

Langstone Channel

6

ENUE
GROVE

A2030

40

Frog Lake

E   Duck Lake   **F**   **52** 68   **G**   **H**   69

101

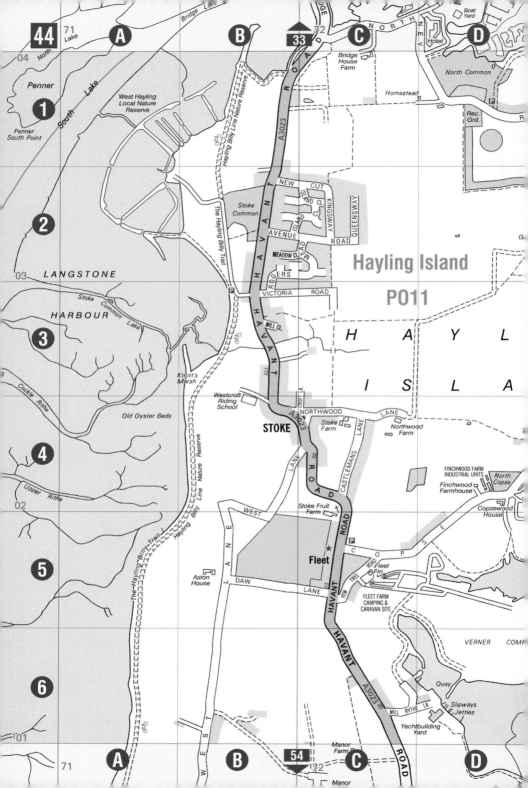

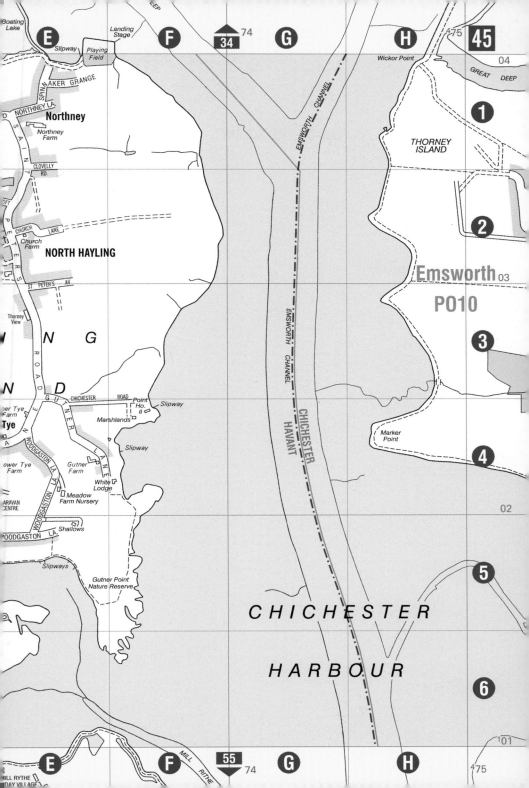

E · **F** · ▲ 74 · **G** · **H** · 475 · **45**

34 · 04

Boating Lake

Landing Stage

Slipway · Playing Field

Wickor Point · GREAT · DEEP

SPINNAKER GRANGE

NORTHNEY LA.

Northney

Northney Farm

❶

THORNEY ISLAND

CLOVELLY RD.

SAINT

CHURCH LANE

Church Farm

NORTH HAYLING

❷

St PETER'S

ST PETER'S AV.

Thorney View

Emsworth 03

PO10

EMSWORTH CHANNEL

N · **G**

ROAD

GUTNER LANE

N · **D**

CHICHESTER ROAD · Point Ho.

Slipway

Marshlands

per Tye Farm

Slipway

WOODGASTON LA.

❸

Tye

Gutner Farm

White Lodge

ower Tye Farm

Meadow Farm Nursery

EMSWORTH CHANNEL

CHICHESTER HAVANT

Marker Point

❹

ARAVAN CENTRE

WOODGASTON LA.

Shallows

WOODGASTON LA.

02

Slipways

Gutner Point Nature Reserve

❺

C H I C H E S T E R

H A R B O U R

❻

101

E · **F** MILL RYTHE · ▼ 55 74 · **G** · **H** · 475

Mill Rythe
DAY VILLAGE

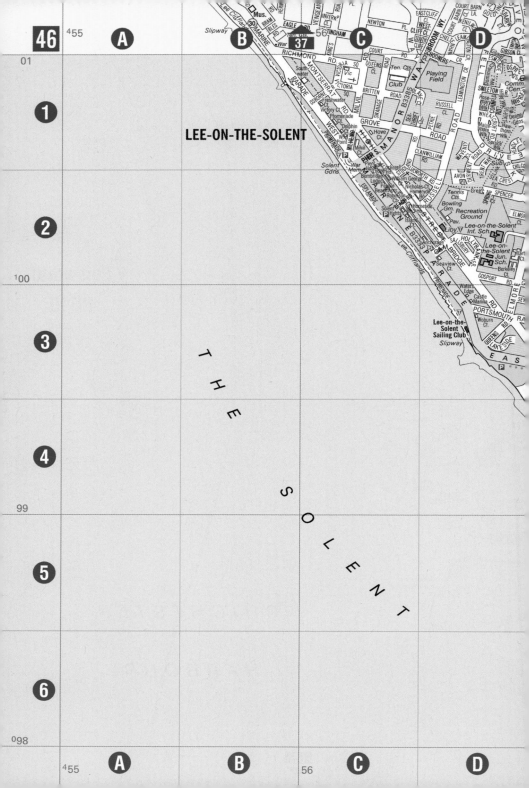

LEE-ON-THE-SOLENT

THE SOLENT

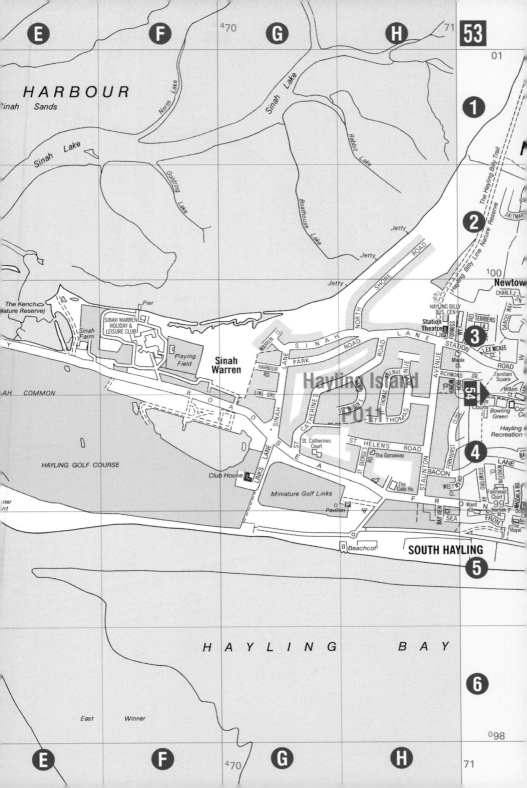

INDEX

Including Streets, Places & Areas, Hospitals etc., Industrial Estates,
Selected Flats & Walkways, Stations and Selected Places of Interest.

HOW TO USE THIS INDEX

1. Each street name is followed by its Postcode District, then by its Locality abbreviation(s) and then by its map reference;
e.g. **Abbeyfield Dr.** Fare . . . .1E **25** is in the PO15 Postcode District and the Fareham Locality and is to be found in square 1E on page **25**.
The page number is shown in bold type.

2. A strict alphabetical order is followed in which Av., Rd., St., etc. (though abbreviated) are read in full and as part of the street name;
e.g. **Apple Gro.** appears after **Applegate Pl.** but before **Appleshaw Grn.**

3. Streets and a selection of flats and walkways that cannot be shown on the mapping, appear in the index with the thoroughfare to which they are connected
shown in brackets; e.g. **Admiral's Cnr.** PO5: S'sea . . . .5D **50** (off Victoria Rd. Sth.)

4. Addresses that are in more than one part are referred to as not continuous.

5. Places and areas are shown in the index in BLUE TYPE and the map reference is to the actual map square in which the town centre or area is located and
not to the place name shown on the map; e.g. **ALVERSTOKE** 5C 48

6. An example of a selected place of interest is Charles Dickens Birthplace Mus. 6G 41

7. Examples of stations are:
Bedhampton Station (Rail) . . . .1D 32; **Fareham Bus Station** . . . .2B 26; **Tipner (Park & Ride)** 2G 41

8. Junction Names are shown in the index in **BOLD CAPITAL TYPE**; e.g. **CAMBRIDGE JUNC.** 5D 4 (3B 50)

9. An example of a Hospital, Hospice or selected Healthcare facility is QUEEN ALEXANDRA HOSPITAL 3B 30

10. Map references for entries that appear on large scale pages **4** & **5** are shown first, with small scale map references shown in brackets;
e.g. **Admiralty Rd.** PO1: Ports 2B **4** (2A **50**)

GENERAL ABBREVIATIONS

All. : Alley	**Flds.** : Fields	**Pde.** : Parade
Apts. : Apartments	**Gdn.** : Garden	**Pk.** : Park
App. : Approach	**Gdns.** : Gardens	**Pas.** : Passage
Arc. : Arcade	**Ga.** : Gate	**Pl.** : Place
Av. : Avenue	**Gt.** : Great	**Pct.** : Precinct
Blvd. : Boulevard	**Grn.** : Green	**Prom.** : Promenade
Bri. : Bridge	**Gro.** : Grove	**Ri.** : Rise
Bldg. : Building	**Hgts.** : Heights	**Rd.** : Road
Bldgs. : Buildings	**Ho.** : House	**Rdbt.** : Roundabout
Bus. : Business	**Ind.** : Industrial	**Shop.** : Shopping
Cvn. : Caravan	**Info.** : Information	**Sth.** : South
Cen. : Centre	**Junc.** : Junction	**Sq.** : Square
Cl. : Close	**La.** : Lane	**St.** : Street
Comn. : Common	**Lit.** : Little	**Ter.** : Terrace
Cnr. : Corner	**Lwr.** : Lower	**Twr.** : Tower
Cotts. : Cottages	**Mnr.** : Manor	**Trad.** : Trading
Ct. : Court	**Mans.** : Mansions	**Up.** : Upper
Cres. : Crescent	**Mkt.** : Market	**Va.** : Vale
Cft. : Croft	**Mdw.** : Meadow	**Vw.** : View
Dr. : Drive	**Mdws.** : Meadows	**Vs.** : Villas
E. : East	**M.** : Mews	**Vis.** : Visitors
Ent. : Enterprise	**Mt.** : Mount	**Wlk.** : Walk
Est. : Estate	**Mus.** : Museum	**W.** : West
Fld. : Field	**Nth.** : North	**Yd.** : Yard

LOCALITY ABBREVIATIONS

Bedhampton: PO9 . . . . .Bed	**Hayling Island**: PO11 . . . . .H Isl	**Southsea**: PO3-5 .S'sea
Blendworth: PO8 .Blen	**Horndean**: PO8 . . . . .Horn	**Southwick**: PO17 . . . . .S'wick
Boarhunt: PO17 . . . . .Boar	**Idsworth**: PO8,PO9 .Ids	**Steep**: GU32 . . . . .Ste
Catherington: PO8 . . . . .Cath	**Knowle Village**: PO15,PO17 . . . . .K Vil	**Stroud**: GU32 . . . . .Stro
Chalton: PO8 . . . . .Chal	**Langstone**: PO9 .Langs	**Stubbington**: PO14 . . . . .Stub
Clanfield: PO8 . . . . .Clan	**Lee-on-the-Solent**: PO13 . . . . .Lee S	**Thorney Island**: PO10 . . . . .T Isl
Cosham: PO6 . . . . .Cosh	**Lovedean**: PO8 .Love	**Titchfield**: PO14,PO15 . . . . .Titch
Cowplain: PO7,PO8 . . . . .Cowp	**North Boarhunt**: PO17 . . . . .N Boa	**Titchfield Common**: PO14 . . . . .Titch C
Denmead: PO7 . . . . .Den	**Petersfield**: GU31-32 . . . . .Pet	**Warblington**: PO9 . . . . .Warb
Drayton: PO6 . . . . .Dray	**Portchester**: PO6,PO16 . . . . .Portc	**Waterlooville**: PO7 . . . . .W'lle
Emsworth: PO9,PO10 . . . . .Ems	**Portsmouth**: PO1-3 . . . . .Ports	**Westbourne**: PO10 . . . . .Westb
Fareham: PO14,PO15,PO16,PO17 . . . . . . .Fare	**Port Solent**: PO6 . . . . .P Sol	**Weston**: GU32 . . . . .W'ton
Farlington: PO6 .Farl	**Purbrook**: PO7 .Purb	**Whiteley**: PO15 . . . . .White
Funtley: PO15,PO16,PO17 . . . . .F'ley	**Rowland's Castle**: PO8,PO9,PO10 . . . . .R Cas	**Wickham**: PO15,PO17 . . . . .Wick
Gosport: PO12,PO13 . . . . .Gos	**Segensworth**: PO15 . . . . .Seg	**Widley**: PO7 . . . . .Wid
Havant: PO7,PO9 . . . . .Hav	**Southbourne**: PO10,PO18 . . . . .S'brne	**Woodmancote**: PO10 . . . . .W'cote

24/7 Fitness
  Fareham 2F 27
  Waterlooville 2G 19

A

Abbas Grn. PO9: Hav 2D **20**	
Abbess Way PO7: W'lle 1H **19**	
Abbeydore Rd. PO6: Cosh 2G **29**	
Abbeyfield Dr. PO15: Fare 1E **25**	

Abbeymede PO6: Cosh 3A **30**	
Abbey Rd. PO15: Fare 1F **25**	
Abbots Cl. PO7: Purb 5E **19**	
Abbotstone Av. PO9: Hav 5G **21**	
Abbots Way PO15: Fare 2F **25**	
A'Becket Ct. PO1: Ports 5C **4** (3A **50**)	
Aberdare Av. PO6: Dray 2D **30**	
Aberdeen Cl. PO15: Fare 6G **13**	
Abingdon Cl. PO12: Gos 3D **48**	
Abrams Way PO9: Hav 2D **32**	
Acacia Gdns. PO8: Horn 2B **10**	
Acacia Lodge PO16: Fare 2B **26**	
Acanthus Ct. PO15: White 1A **12**	
Access Point PO6: Cosh 4A **30**	

Acer Way PO9: Hav 5H **21**	
Ackworth Rd. PO3: Ports 6C **30**	
Acorn Bus. Cen. PO6: Cosh 4H **29**	
Acorn Cl. PO6: Farl 3H **31**	
PO13: Gos 4D **38**	
Acorn Dr. PO8: Horn 1D **10**	
Acorn Gdns. PO8: Horn 1B **10**	
The Acorns PO7: Den 3C **8**	
PO9: Hav 6F **21**	
Acre La. PO7: W'lle 6C **10**	
Action Stations Exhibition Mus. . . .2B **4** (2A **50**)	
Adair Rd. PO4: S'sea 5G **51**	
Adames Rd. PO1: Ports 1E **51**	
Adderbury Av. PO10: Ems 6D **22**	

Addison Rd. PO4: S'sea 4E 51
Adelaide Pl. PO16: Fare 2C 26
Adhurst Rd. PO9: Hav 5G 21
Admiral Ho. PO12: Gos 2F 49
The Admiral Pk. PO3: Ports 2C 42
Admiral Pl. PO16: Portc 3H 27
The Admirals PO1: Ports 4B 4
Admiral's Cnr. PO5: S'sea 5D 50
　　　　　　　　(off Victoria Rd. Sth.)
Admirals Ct. PO5: S'sea 5C 50
Admirals Ho. PO4: S'sea 3H 51
Admirals Pl. PO6: Cosh 3B 30
Admiral Sq. PO5: S'sea 4C 50
　　　　　　　　　(off Nelson Rd.)
Admiral's Wlk. PO1: Ports 1A 4 (1H 49)
Admirals Wlk. PO12: Gos 4B 48
Admiralty Cl. PO12: Gos 6A 40
Admiralty Rd. PO1: Ports 2B 4 (2A 50)
　　PO12: Gos 5G 49
Admiralty Twr. PO1: Ports ...2B 4 (2A 50)
Adsdean Cl. PO9: Hav 5E 21
Adstone La. PO3: Ports 1E 43
Adur Cl. PO12: Gos 6F 39
Aerial Rd. PO17: S'wick 1F 29
Aerodrome Rd. PO13: Gos 1D 38
Agincourt Rd. PO2: Ports 6H 41
Agnew Ho. PO12: Gos 1D 48
Agnew Rd. PO13: Gos 2C 38
Ainsdale Rd. PO6: Dray 2F 31
Aintree Dr. PO7: W'lle 6B 10
Airport Ind. Est. PO3: Ports 2D 42
Airport Service Rd. PO3: Ports ..1C 42
Airspeed Rd. PO3: Ports 3E 43
Ajax Cl. PO14: Stub 4F 37
Akela Way PO10: Westb 5F 23
Alameda Rd. PO7: Purb 5F 19
Alameda Way PO7: Purb 5F 19
Alan Gro. PO15: Fare 1G 25
Albacore Cl. PO13: Lee S 2E 47
Albany Cvn. Site 4F 37
Albany Rd. PO12: Gos 3D 48
Albany Rd. PO5: S'sea 6H 5 (4D 50)
　　PO13: Gos 6D 38
Albatross Wlk. PO13: Gos 3B 38
Albemarle Av. PO12: Gos 6H 39
Albert Gro. PO5: S'sea 4D 50
Albert Rd. PO4: S'sea 4D 50
　　PO5: S'sea 4D 50
　　PO6: Cosh 4B 30
　　PO14: Fare 3H 37
Albert St. PO12: Gos 2E 49
Albion Cl. PO16: Portc 5H 27
Albretia Av. PO8: Cowp 4F 9
Alchorne Rd. PO3: Ports 2D 42
Alderfield GU32: Pet 4C 56
Alder La. PO12: Gos 2H 47
Alderman Gdns. PO3: Ports 1G 51
Aldermoor Rd. PO7: Purb 5F 19
　　PO13: Gos 6D 38
Aldermoor Rd. E. PO7: Purb 4F 19
Aldershot Ho. PO9: Hav 4H 21
Alders Rd. PO16: Fare 4B 26
Alderwood Cl. PO9: Bed 6B 20
Aldrich Rd. PO1: Ports 1A 50
Aldridge Cl. PO8: Clan 2G 7
Aldroke St. PO6: Cosh 4B 30
ALDSWORTH 3G 23
Aldsworth Cl. PO6: Dray 3E 31
Aldsworth Comn. Rd. PO10: Westb ..4G 23
Aldsworth Gdns. PO6: Dray 3E 31
Aldsworth Path 3E 31
Aldwell St. PO5: S'sea 4H 5 (3D 50)
Alec Rose Ho. PO12: Gos 3E 49
Alec Rose La. PO1: Ports 3F 5 (2C 50)
Alecto Rd. PO12: Gos 4D 48
Alencon Cl. PO12: Gos 5A 40
Alexander Cl. PO7: W'lle 4F 19
Alexander Gro. PO16: Fare 3A 26
Alexandra Av. PO11: H Isl 5B 54
Alexandra Ct. PO4: S'sea 6E 51
　　　　　　　　(off Sth. Pde.)
Alexandra Rd. PO1: Ports 1H 5 (1D 50)
Alexandra St. PO12: Gos 1C 48
Alexandria Pk. PO9: Hav 4D 32
Alex McKee Cl. PO11: H Isl 3A 54
Alex Way PO2: Ports 2H 41
Alfred Rd. PO1: Ports 2E 5 (2B 50)
　　PO14: Stub 2F 37
Alfrey Cl. PO10: S'brne 3G 35
Algiers Rd. PO3: Ports 5D 42
Alhambra Rd. PO4: S'sea 6E 51
Allaway Av. PO6: Cosh 3D 28
Allbrook Ct. PO9: Hav 3D 20
Allcot Rd. PO3: Ports 3B 42

Allenby Gro. PO16: Portc 4A 28
Allenby Rd. PO7: Purb 3E 19
　　PO12: Gos 1A 48
Allendale Av. PO10: Ems 6C 22
Allen's Rd. PO4: S'sea 5E 51
Alliance Cl. PO13: Gos 4D 38
Alliance Ho. PO1: Ports 1E 51
Alliance Way PO3: Ports 2F 51
Allmara Dr. PO7: W'lle 5H 19
All Saint's Rd. PO1: Ports 6H 41
All Saints St. PO1: Ports 1C 50
Alma St. PO12: Gos 1C 48
Alma Ter. PO4: S'sea 4G 51
Almond Cl. PO8: Horn 3C 10
　　PO9: Bed 3H 31
Almondsbury Rd. PO6: Cosh 1D 28
Almondside PO13: Gos 4E 39
Alphage Rd. PO12: Gos 4F 39
Alpine Cres. PO14: Titch C 2A 24
Alresford Rd. PO9: Hav 5E 21
Alsford Rd. PO7: Purb 4F 19
Alston Rd. PO7: W'lle 5E 9
Althorpe Dr. PO3: Ports 1E 43
Alton Gro. PO16: Portc 5A 28
Alum Way PO16: Fare 2E 27
Alvara Rd. PO12: Gos 5C 48
Alver Bri. Vw. PO12: Gos 4D 48
Alvercliffe Dr. PO12: Gos 5B 48
Alver Quay PO12: Gos 4D 48
Alver Rd. PO1: Ports 1E 51
　　PO12: Gos 3D 48
　　　　　　　(not continuous)
ALVERSTOKE 5C 48
Alverstoke Ct. PO12: Gos 5C 48
Alverstoke Lawn Tennis, Squash &
　Badminton Club 4C 48
　　　(within Alverstoke Sports Club)
Alverstoke Sports Club 4C 48
Alverstone Rd. PO4: S'sea 2G 51
Alveston Av. PO14: Fare 3F 25
Amaryllis Cl. PO15: Seg 5A 12
Amberley Ct. PO14: Stub 4F 37
　　PO17: K Vil 2G 13
　　　　　　　(off Knowle Av.)
Amberley Rd. PO2: Ports 2B 42
　　PO8: Clan 2H 7
　　PO12: Gos 5G 39
Ambleside Ct. PO12: Gos 6C 48
Ameiva Point PO3: Ports 3D 42
Amelia Gdns. PO13: Gos 2H 47
Amersham Cl. PO12: Gos 3A 48
Amey Ind. Est. GU32: Pet 4C 56
Ampfield Cl. PO9: Hav 5B 20
Amport Ct. PO9: Hav 3D 20
Amyas Ct. PO4: S'sea 3A 52
The Anchorage PO12: Gos 3E 49
Anchorage Pk. PO3: Ports 2E 43
Anchorage Rd. PO3: Ports 1D 42
Anchor Ct. PO11: H Isl 6F 55
Anchor Ga. Rd. PO1: Ports 1C 4 (1A 50)
Anchor La. PO1: Ports 2A 4 (2H 49)
Anderson Ct. PO9: Hav 6G 21
Andover Ho. PO9: Hav 4G 21
Andover Rd. PO4: S'sea 5F 51
Andrew Bell St. PO1: Ports 1C 50
Andrew Cl. PO3: Ports 1F 51
Andrew Cres. PO7: W'lle 5F 9
Andrew Pl. PO14: Stub 3D 36
Angela Ct. PO9: Hav 5F 21
Angelica Ct. PO7: W'lle 3A 20
Angelica Way PO15: White 1A 12
Angelo Cl. PO7: W'lle 1A 20
Angelus Cl. PO14: Stub 3E 37
Angerstein Rd. PO2: Ports 4H 41
Anglesea Rd. PO1: Ports 2E 5 (2B 50)
　　PO13: Lee S 3E 47
ANGLESEY 6D 48
Anglesey Arms Rd. PO12: Gos 5C 48
Anglesey Rd. PO12: Gos 6C 48
Anglesey Vw. PO12: Gos 4D 48
Angmering Ho. PO1: Ports 2G 5 (2C 50)
Angus Cl. PO15: Fare 6G 13
Angus Way PO7: W'lle 6E 9
Anjou Cres. PO15: Fare 1F 25
Anker La. PO14: Stub 1E 37
Ankerwyke PO13: Gos 4B 38
ANMORE 3D 8
Anmore Cl. PO9: Hav 5D 20
Anmore Dr. PO7: W'lle 5F 9
Anmore La. PO7: Den 3D 8
Anmore Rd. PO7: Den 3C 8

Anne Cres. PO7: W'lle 3G 19
Annes Ct. PO11: H Isl 5A 54
ANN'S HILL 3C 48
Ann's Hill Rd. PO12: Gos 1C 48
Anson Cl. PO9: Bed 2B 32
　　PO13: Gos 2H 47
Anson Ct. PO1: Ports 4B 4 (3A 50)
Anson Gro. PO16: Portc 2B 28
Anson Rd. PO4: S'sea 2G 51
Anstice Ct. PO13: Lee S 1D 46
ANTHILL COMMON 2A 8
Anthony Gro. PO12: Gos 4F 39
Anthony Way PO10: Ems 6D 22
Antigua Pl. PO6: Cosh 1D 28
Anvil Cl. PO7: W'lle 6C 10
Anvil Ct. PO4: S'sea 3H 51
Anzac Cl. PO14: Stub 1E 37
Apex Cen. PO14: Fare 6A 26
Apollo Cl. PO5: S'sea 5G 5 (3D 50)
Apollo Dr. PO7: Purb 6C 10
Applegate Pl. PO8: Horn 1A 10
Apple Gro. PO10: S'brne 3F 35
Appleshaw Grn. PO9: Hav 5C 20
Appleton Cl. PO8: Clan 2H 7
Appleton Rd. PO15: Fare 1D 24
Appletree Ho. PO7: W'lle 2G 19
　　　　　　　(off Hambledon Rd.)
Applewood Gro. PO7: Wid 6E 19
Applewood Rd. PO9: Bed 6C 20
The Approach PO3: Ports 4C 42
April Sq. PO1: Ports 1H 5 (1D 50)
Apsley Rd. PO4: S'sea 3G 51
Archer Ho. PO12: Gos 6E 49
Archery La. PO16: Fare 1C 26
Arden Cl. PO12: Gos 3B 48
Ardington Ri. PO7: Purb 6G 19
Arethusa Ho. PO1: Ports 5B 4 (3A 50)
Argyle Cres. PO15: Fare 1G 25
Ariel Rd. PO1: Ports 2E 51
Arismore Ct. PO13: Lee S 6F 37
Ark Royal Cres. PO13: Lee S 6G 37
Arle Cl. PO8: Clan 1C 6
Arminers Cl. PO12: Gos 6D 48
Armory La. PO1: Ports 5C 4 (3A 50)
Armstrong Cl. PO7: W'lle 5F 9
　　PO12: Gos 6E 49
Arnaud Cl. PO2: Ports 6H 41
Arnside Rd. PO7: W'lle 1G 19
Arragon Ct. PO7: W'lle 1A 20
Arran Cl. PO6: Cosh 2B 30
Arras Ho. PO15: Fare 1E 25
Arras Rd. PO3: Ports 6B 30
Arreton Ct. PO12: Gos 2C 48
Arthur Dann Ct. PO6: Cosh 4A 30
Arthur Kille Ho. PO7: W'lle 3F 19
Arthur Pope Ho. PO5: S'sea ...4H 5 (3D 50)
Artillery Cl. PO6: Cosh 2G 29
Artillery Ter. PO4: S'sea 3H 51
Art Space Portsmouth 5G 5 (3C 50)
Arun Cl. GU31: Pet 5C 56
　　PO8: Cowp 4A 10
Arundel Ct. PO5: S'sea 6D 50
　　　　　　　(off Sth. Parade)
Arundel Dr. PO16: Fare 1A 26
Arundel Rd. PO12: Gos 2B 48
Arundel St. PO1: Ports 2F 5 (2C 50)
Ascot Rd. PO3: Ports 6C 42
Ashburton Ct. PO5: S'sea 5C 50
　　　　　　　(off Ashburton Rd.)
Ashburton Rd. PO5: S'sea 5C 50
　　PO12: Gos 5B 48
Ashby Pl. PO5: S'sea 5C 50
Ashdown PO13: Gos 4D 38
Ashe Rd. PO9: Hav 4H 21
Ashford Cl. PO6: Cosh 2A 30
Ashington Cl. PO8: Cowp 3A 10
Ashlett Lawn PO9: Hav 3D 20
Ashley Cl. PO8: Love 2H 9
　　PO9: Hav 5D 20
Ashley Ct. PO12: Gos 2C 48
Ashley Down La. PO17: Boar 3H 15
Ashley Wlk. 4C 30
Ashling Cl. PO7: Den 3B 8
Ashling Gdns. PO7: Den 3B 8
Ashling La. PO2: Ports 4H 41
Ashling Pk. Rd. PO7: Den 3B 8

Ashtead Cl.—Belmont Pl.

Ashtead Cl. PO15: Fare .2E **25**
Ashmead Arc. PO7: W'lle .2F **19**
Ashtead Cl. PO16: Portc .3G **27**
Ashton Way PO14: Stub .5F **37**
Ashurst Ct. PO12: Gos .4H **47**
Ashurst Rd. PO6: Cosh .3A **30**
Ash Way PO15: White .1A **12**
Ashwood PO15: White .4A **12**
Ashwood Cl. PO9: Bed .5B **20**
PO11: H Isl .4C **54**
Ashwood Lodge *PO16: Fare .1B 26*
(off Southampton Rd.)
Ashworth Ho. *PO12: Gos .6B 40*
(off Searle Dr.)
Aspengrove PO13: Gos .4E **39**
Aspen Way PO8: Horn .2A **10**
Aspex Art Gallery .4B **4** (3A **50**)
Assheton Ct. PO16: Portc .4B **28**
Astley St. PO5: S'sea .5E **5** (3C **50**)
Aston Rd. PO4: S'sea .4F **51**
PO7: W'lle .6F **9**
Astra Wlk. PO12: Gos .3F **49**
Astrid Cl. PO11: H Isl .4E **55**
Atalanta Cl. PO4: S'sea .2A **52**
Athena Av. PO7: Purb .6H **19**
Athens Way PO7: Purb .5G **19**
Atherley Rd. PO11: H Isl .2A **54**
Atherstone Wlk. .5F **5** (3C **50**)
Atkinson Cl. PO12: Gos .5C **48**
Atkinson Ct. PO6: Cosh .3C **30**
Atkins Pl. PO15: Fare .6E **13**
Atlantis Av. PO7: Purb .1G **31**
Aubin Wood PO10: Ems .5C **22**
Aubrey Cl. PO11: H Isl .3A **54**
Auckland Rd. E. PO5: S'sea .5C **50**
Auckland Rd. W. PO5: S'sea .5C **50**
Audley Ct. PO16: Fare .2F **27**
Audret Cl. PO16: Portc .5H **27**
Auger Way PO7: W'lle .6E **9**
Augustine Rd. PO6: Dray .2E **31**
Auriol Dr. PO9: Bed .3H **31**
Aurora Ho. PO7: W'lle .2G **19**
Austerberry Way PO13: Gos .5E **39**
Austin Ct. PO6: Cosh .2F **29**
Australia Cl. PO1: Ports .2H **5** (2D **50**)
Aust Rd. PO14: Fare .3F **25**
Avalon Ct. PO10: Ems .1D **34**
Avalon Ho. PO1: Ports .2F **5** (2C **50**)
The Avenue GU31: Pet .4D **56**
PO12: Gos .5C **48**
PO14: Fare .3D **24**
Avenue Ct. PO12: Gos .5C **48**
Avenue De Caen PO5: S'sea .6C **50**
Avenue Lawn Tennis & Squash Club .2H **33**
Avenue Rd. PO11: H Isl .2B **44**
PO12: Gos .2E **49**
PO14: Fare .2H **25**
Avery La. PO12: Gos .6F **39**
Avington Grn. PO9: Hav .3H **21**
Avocet Cl. PO4: S'sea .2H **51**
Avocet Ho. PO4: S'sea .2H **51**
Avocet Quay PO10: S'brne .4E **35**
Avocet Wlk. PO13: Gos .3A **38**
Avocet Way PO8: Horn .6A **6**
Avon Cl. GU31: Pet .6C **56**
PO13: Lee S .2D **46**
Avon Ct. PO8: Cowp .3H **9**
Avondale Rd. PO1: Ports .1F **51**
PO7: W'lle .1H **19**
Avon Wlk. PO16: Portc .3G **27**
Awbridge Rd. PO9: Hav .5C **20**
Axis Pk. PO14: Fare .5A **26**
Aylen Rd. PO3: Ports .3C **42**
Aylesbury Rd. PO2: Ports .5B **42**
Ayling Cl. PO13: Gos .6C **38**
Aylward St. PO1: Ports .2C **4** (2A **50**)
Ayrshire Rd. PO7: W'lle .6D **8**
Aysgarth Rd. PO7: W'lle .1G **19**
Azalea Cl. PO9: Hav .5A **22**

B

Back La. PO17: S'wick .3C **16**
Bacon La. PO11: H Isl .4H **53**
Baddesley Gdns. PO9: Hav .3D **20**
Bader Way PO15: White .4B **12**
Badger Brow PO7: W'lle .3A **20**
Badger Cl. PO15: Fare .1F **25**
Badger Rd. PO14: Fare .6H **25**
BAFFINS .6C **42**
Baffins Rd. PO3: Ports .1G **51**
Bagot Ho. PO12: Gos .6F **39**
Bailey Rd. PO9: R Cas .6H **11**
Bailey's Rd. PO5: S'sea .4H **5** (3D **50**)
Baker St. PO1: Ports .6H **41**
Balchin Ho. PO1: Ports .2C **4**
Balderton Cl. PO2: Ports .1B **42**
Baler La. PO7: W'lle .6E **9**
Balfour Cl. PO13: Gos .1H **47**
Balfour Rd. PO2: Ports .4A **42**
Ballard Ct. PO12: Gos .3D **48**
Balliol Rd. PO2: Ports .5A **42**
Balmoral Cl. PO13: Gos .3D **38**
Balmoral Ct. PO5: S'sea .6C **50**
Balmoral Dr. PO7: Purb .5E **19**
Balmoral Rd. PO15: Fare .6G **13**
Balmoral Way GU32: Pet .3D **56**
Bankside PO12: Gos .5B **48**
Bannerman Rd. GU32: Pet .3D **56**
Bapaume Rd. PO3: Ports .6B **30**
Barbastelle Ho. PO10: Ems .5D **22**
Barbastelle Wlk. PO17: K Vil .2F **13**
Barbican M. PO16: Portc .4C **28**
Barclay Ho. *PO12: Gos .3G 49*
(off Trinity Grn.)
Bardon Way PO14: Fare .3F **25**
Barentin Way GU31: Pet .2E **57**
Barfleur Cl. PO15: Fare .1F **25**
Barfleur Rd. PO14: Fare .6A **26**
Barham Cl. PO12: Gos .1D **48**
Barham Rd. GU32: Pet .4D **56**
Barham Way PO2: Ports .1H **41**
Barkis Ho. PO1: Ports .6H **41**
Barley Ri. PO8: Horn .6D **6**
Barlow Cl. PO14: Stub .3D **36**
Barn Cl. PO10: Ems .3B **34**
PO14: Titch .4B **24**
Barncroft Way PO9: Hav .5D **20**
Barnes Rd. PO1: Ports .1E **51**
Barnes Wallis Rd. PO15: Seg .5A **12**
Barnes Way PO9: Bed .6D **20**
Barney Evans Cres. PO8: Cowp .4F **9**
Barnfield Cl. PO10: S'brne .2H **35**
Barnfield Ct. PO14: Fare .3G **25**
Barnfield Rd. GU31: Pet .4G **57**
Barn Fold PO7: W'lle .6B **10**
Barn Grn. Cl. PO7: Den .3B **8**
Barnwood Rd. PO15: Fare .2F **25**
Baroda Ct. PO2: Ports .5H **41**
Baronsmere Ct. PO12: Gos .3C **48**
Barracks Rd. PO4: S'sea .5A **52**
Barrel M. PO8: Horn .6D **6**
Barrington Ho. PO2: Ports .6H **41**
Barrington Ter. PO5: S'sea .6F **5**
Barrita Cl. PO12: Gos .2C **48**
Bartlett Cl. PO15: Fare .6G **13**
Bartlett Ct. PO13: Lee S .2D **46**
Barton Cross PO8: Horn .6B **6**
Barton Gro. PO3: Ports .2D **42**
Bartons Ct. PO12: Gos .2D **48**
Bartons Rd. PO9: Hav .4G **21**
Barwell Gro. PO10: Ems .6C **22**
Barwell La. PO13: Gos .6C **26**
Basing Rd. PO9: Hav .4E **21**
Basin St. PO2: Ports .5H **41**
Bassett Wlk. PO9: Hav .3D **20**
Bateson Hall PO1: Ports .3F **5**
Bath & Wells Ct. PO13: Gos .1G **47**
Bathing La. PO1: Ports .5A **4** (4H **49**)
Bath La. PO16: Fare .2C **26**
Bath La. Cotts. PO16: Fare .3C **26**
Bath La. Lwr. PO16: Fare .2C **26**
Bath Rd. PO4: S'sea .4F **51**
PO10: Ems .4D **34**
Bath Sq. PO1: Ports .5A **4** (3H **49**)
Bathurst Cl. PO11: H Isl .4A **54**
Bathurst Way PO2: Ports .3F **41**
Battenburg Av. PO2: Ports .3A **42**
Battenburg Rd. PO12: Gos .2E **49**
Battens Way PO9: Hav .5F **21**
Battery Cl. PO12: Gos .5F **39**
Battery Prom. .6A **4** (4H **49**)
Battery Row PO1: Ports .6B **4** (4A **50**)
Baybridge Rd. PO9: Hav .4H **21**
Bayfields *PO5: S'sea .5C 50*
(off Shaftesbury Rd.)
Bayly Av. PO16: Portc .5B **28**
Bayntun Dr. PO13: Lee S .6G **37**
Bay Rd. PO12: Gos .4B **48**
Bayswater Ho. PO5: S'sea .4D **50**
Baythorn Cl. PO2: Ports .6H **41**
Bay Tree Lodge PO14: Stub .3F **37**
Bay Vw. Ct. PO11: H Isl .5H **53**
Beach Ct. PO11: H Isl .6F **55**
Beach Dr. PO6: Cosh .3D **28**
Beaches Rd. PO17: S'wick .3E **17**
Beach Rd. PO5: S'sea .6D **50**
PO10: Ems .3C **34**
PO11: H Isl .4A **54**
PO13: Lee S .2C **46**
Beachway PO16: Portc .5B **28**
Beacon Ho. *PO5: S'sea .2D 50*
(in Cumberland Bus. Cen.)
Beaconsfield Av. PO6: Cosh .4C **30**
Beaconsfield Rd. PO7: W'lle .1G **19**
PO16: Fare .3B **26**
Beacon Sq. PO10: Ems .3C **34**
Beamond Ct. PO6: Cosh .4C **30**
Beasant Cl. PO3: Ports .1H **51**
Beatrice Rd. PO4: S'sea .5E **51**
Beatty Dr. PO12: Gos .5B **48**
Beatty Ho. PO1: Ports .1H **5**
Beauchamp Av. PO13: Gos .3C **38**
Beaufort Av. PO16: Fare .6H **13**
Beaufort Cl. PO13: Lee S .1E **47**
Beaufort Rd. PO5: S'sea .6D **50**
PO9: Bed .1D **32**
Beaulieu Av. PO9: Hav .3D **20**
PO16: Portc .3G **27**
Beaulieu Ct. *PO8: Cowp .3H 9*
(off Crombie Cl.)
Beaulieu Pl. PO13: Gos .3C **38**
Beaulieu Rd. PO2: Ports .4A **42**
Beaumont Cl. PO15: Fare .6F **13**
Beaumont Ct. PO12: Gos .5G **39**
Beaumont Ri. PO15: Fare .5F **13**
Beckham La. GU32: Pet .3B **56**
Beckless Av. PO8: Clan .2H **7**
Beck St. PO1: Ports .2D **4** (2B **50**)
BEDENHAM .1D **38**
Bedenham La. PO13: Gos .2D **38**
(not continuous)
Bedford Cl. PO9: Warb .3H **33**
Bedford Dr. PO14: Titch C .3A **24**
Bedford Rd. GU32: Pet .3B **56**
Bedford St. PO5: S'sea .4F **5** (3C **50**)
PO12: Gos .1C **48**
BEDHAMPTON .1C **32**
Bedhampton Hill PO9: Bed .2A **32**
(not continuous)
Bedhampton Ho. PO1: Ports .1H **5**
Bedhampton Rd. PO2: Ports .5B **42**
PO9: Bed .1C **32**
Bedhampton Station (Rail) .1D **32**
Bedhampton Way PO9: Hav .5F **21**
Beecham Rd. PO1: Ports .6A **42**
Beech Cl. PO8: Cowp .5H **9**
Beechcroft Cl. PO15: Fare .2D **24**
Beechcroft Rd. PO12: Gos .4C **48**
The Beeches PO7: W'lle .1H **19**
Beech Gro. PO11: H Isl .3D **54**
PO12: Gos .4C **48**
Beech Rd. PO8: Clan .2G **7**
PO15: Fare .1G **25**
Beech Way PO8: Horn .2B **10**
Beechwood Av. PO7: W'lle .3G **19**
Beechwood Lodge PO16: Fare .1B **26**
Beechwood Rd. PO2: Ports .1A **42**
Beechworth Rd. PO9: Hav .2F **33**
Beehive Ter. PO6: Cosh .2G **29**
Beehive Wlk. PO1: Ports .5C **4** (3A **50**)
Bee Orchid Cl. PO8: Clan .2H **7**
Beeston Ct. *PO1: Ports .6A 42*
(off Belmore Cl.)
Behrendt Cl. PO12: Gos .1C **48**
Behrendt Ho. *PO12: Gos .1C 48*
(off Behrendt Cl.)
Belgravia Rd. PO2: Ports .4B **42**
Belham Apts. PO2: Ports .4A **42**
Bellair Ho. PO9: Hav .2G **33**
Bellair Rd. PO9: Hav .2G **33**
Bell Cres. PO7: W'lle .3G **19**
Bell Davies Rd. PO14: Stub .4D **36**
Bellevue La. PO10: Ems .1D **34**
Bellevue Ter. PO5: S'sea .6E **5** (4B **50**)
BELLFIELD .4B **24**
Bellfield PO14: Titch .4B **24**
Bellflower Way PO15: Titch .6B **12**
BELL HILL .2C **56**
Bell Hill GU32: Pet .1C **56**
Bell Hill Ridge GU32: Pet .2C **56**
Bellinger Ho. PO9: Bed .2D **32**
Bell Rd. PO6: Cosh .3H **29**
Bells La. PO14: Stub .3E **37**
Belmont Cl. PO8: Horn .2C **6**
PO14: Stub .2F **37**
Belmont Gdns. PO11: H Isl .6F **55**
Belmont Pl. PO9: Bed .1C **32**

Belmont Junc.—Brecon Ho.

BELMONT JUNC. **1C 32**
Belmont Pl. PO5: S'sea 6G **5** (4C **50**)
Belmont St. PO5: S'sea 6G **5** (4C **50**)
Belmore Cl. PO1: Ports 6A **42**
Belney La. PO7: Den 2H **17**
PO17: S'wick .2H **17**
Belvedere Pl. GU32: Pet 3D **56**
Belvoir Cl. PO16: Fare 2A **26**
Bembridge Ct. PO11: H Isl 6E **55**
Bembridge Cres. PO4: S'sea 6E **51**
Bembridge Dr. PO11: H Isl 6E **55**
Bembridge Ho. PO11: H Isl 5D **54**
Bembridge Lodge PO13: Lee S 2C **46**
Bemister's La. PO12: Gos 3G **49**
Benbow Cl. PO8: Horn 6C **6**
Benbow Ho. PO1: Ports 2B **4**
Benbow Pl. PO1: Ports 2B **4** (2A **50**)
Benedict Way PO16: Portc 2C **28**
Beneficial St. PO1: Ports 2B **4** (2A **50**)
Benham Dr. PO3: Ports 1B **42**
Benham Gro. PO16: Portc 5B **28**
Bentham Rd. PO12: Gos 4D **48**
Bentley Cl. PO8: Horn 5C **6**
Bentley Ct. PO9: Hav 4H **21**
Bentley Cres. PO16: Fare 1H **25**
Bentworth Cl. PO9: Hav 5D **20**
Bepton Down GU31: Pet 4E **57**
Bere Farm La. PO17: N Boa 2F **15**
Bere La. PO17: K Vil 2G **13**
Bere Rd. PO7: Den 3B **8**
Beresford Cl. PO7: W'lle 3G **19**
Beresford Rd. PO2: Ports 4A **42**
PO14: Stub 2F **37**
The Berkeley *PO4: S'sea 6E **51***
(off Sth. Pde.)
Berkeley Cl. PO14: Stub 3D **36**
Berkeley Ct. PO13: Lee S 2D **46**
Berkeley Sq. PO9: Warb 2H **33**
Berkshire Cl. PO1: Ports 2D **50**
Bermuda Ho. PO6: Cosh 1D **28**
Bernard Av. PO6: Cosh 3C **30**
Bernard Powell Ho. PO9: Hav 2G **33**
Berney Rd. PO4: S'sea 3A **52**
Bernina Av. PO7: W'lle 5E **9**
Bernina Cl. PO7: W'lle 5E **9**
Berrydown Rd. PO9: Hav 2C **20**
Berry La. PO14: Stub 3C **36**
Berry Mdw. Cotts. PO17: S'wick 3C **16**
Bertie Rd. PO4: S'sea 3H **51**
Berwyn Wlk. PO14: Fare 3G **25**
Beryl Av. PO12: Gos 5F **39**
Beryton Cl. PO12: Gos 1C **48**
Beryton Rd. PO12: Gos 1C **48**
Bettesworth Rd. PO1: Ports 6A **42**
Betula Cl. PO7: W'lle 3A **20**
Beulam Ct. PO7: W'lle 6D **8**
Bevan Rd. PO8: Cowp 2H **9**
Beverley Cvn. Pk. 5G **55**
Beverley Gro. PO6: Farl 2H **31**
Beverley Rd. PO14: Stub 4E **37**
Beverly Cl. PO13: Gos 3D **38**
Beverston Rd. PO6: Cosh 2E **29**
Bevis Rd. PO2: Ports 4H **41**
PO12: Gos 2D **48**
Bevis Rd. Nth. PO2: Ports 4H **41**
Bickton Wlk. PO9: Hav 3D **20**
Bidbury La. PO9: Bed 2C **32**
Biddlecombe Cl. PO13: Gos 5C **38**
Biggin Wlk. PO14: Fare 3G **25**
Bilberry Av. PO8: Clan 2H **7**
Billett Av. PO7: W'lle 6H **9**
Billing Cl. PO4: S'sea 4H **51**
Billington Ct. *PO1: Ports 2E **51***
(off Walmer Rd.)
Bill Sargent Cres. PO1: Ports 1E **51**
Bill Stillwell Ct. PO2: Ports 3G **41**
Billy Lawn Av. PO9: Hav 4F **21**
Billy Rd. PO11: H Isl 3A **54**
Billys Copse PO9: Hav 4E **21**
Bilton Bus. Pk. PO3: Ports 2E **43**
Bilton Way PO3: Ports 3E **43**
The Binnacle Cvn. Pk. 5G **55**
Binnacle Way PO6: Cosh 3F **29**
Binness Path PO6: Farl 4G **31**
Binness Way PO6: Farl 4G **31**
Binsteed Rd. PO2: Ports 5A **42**
Birch Cl. PO8: Cowp 4G **9**
Birch Dr. PO13: Gos 1C **38**
Birchmore Cl. PO13: Gos 3C **38**
Birch Tree Cl. PO10: Ems 5D **22**
Birch Tree Dr. PO10: Ems 5D **22**
Birchwood Lodge *PO16: Fare 1B **26***
(off Southampton Rd.)
Birdham Rd. PO11: H Isl 5G **55**
Birdlip Cl. PO8: Horn 1A **10**
Birdlip Rd. PO6: Cosh 2F **29**
Birdwood Gro. PO16: Portc 3F **27**
Birkdale Av. PO6: Dray 2E **31**
Biscay Cl. PO14: Stub 2D **36**
Bishop Crispian Way PO1: Ports 2E **5** (2B **50**)
Bishopsfield Rd. PO14: Fare 4G **25**
Bishopstoke Rd. PO9: Hav 4E **21**
Bishop St. PO1: Ports 2C **4** (2A **50**)
Bishops Wood PO14: Fare 3H **25**
Bittern Cl. PO12: Gos 6H **39**
Bitterne Cl. PO9: Hav 3F **21**
Blackberry Cl. PO8: Clan 1D **6**
Blackbird Cl. PO8: Cowp 3H **9**
Blackbird Way PO13: Lee S 6H **37**
Blackbrook Bus. Pk. PO15: Fare 2G **25**
Blackbrook Ho. Dr. PO14: Fare 2G **25**
Blackbrook Pk. Av. PO15: Fare 2G **25**
Blackbrook Rd. PO15: Fare 1E **25**
Blackburn Ct. PO13: Gos 2H **47**
Blackcap Cl. PO9: R Cas 6G **11**
Blackdown Cres. PO9: Hav 5E **21**
Blackfriars Cl. PO5: S'sea 4H **5** (3D **50**)
Blackfriars Rd. PO5: S'sea 3H **5** (2D **50**)
Blackhouse La. PO17: N Boa 1G **15**
Blackmoor Wlk. PO9: Hav 4H **21**
Blackthorn Dr. PO11: H Isl 4E **55**
PO12: Gos 4G **39**
Blackthorn Rd. PO11: H Isl 4E **55**
Blackthorn Ter. PO1: Ports 1C **4** (1B **50**)
Blackthorn Wlk. *PO7: W'lle 6B **10***
(off Grassmere Way)
Blackwater Cl. PO6: Cosh 3H **29**
Blackwood Ho. PO1: Ports 6H **41**
Bladon Cl. PO9: Hav 6A **22**
Blake Ct. PO12: Gos 3G **49**
Blake Ho. PO1: Ports 4A **4** (3H **49**)
Blakemere Cres. PO6: Cosh 2G **29**
Blake Rd. PO1: Ports 6D **40**
PO6: Farl 2F **31**
PO12: Gos 2E **49**
Blakesley La. PO3: Ports 1E **43**
Blanchard Av. PO13: Gos 2H **47**
Blankney Cl. PO14: Stub 3D **36**
Blaven Wlk. PO14: Fare 3G **25**
BLENDWORTH **5E 7**
Blendworth Cres. PO9: Hav 6E **21**
Blendworth Ho. PO1: Ports 1H **5**
Blendworth La. PO8: Blen 6D **6**
Blendworth Rd. PO4: S'sea 2H **51**
Blenheim Ct. PO4: S'sea 4G **51**
Blenheim Gdns. PO9: Hav 1H **33**
PO12: Gos 5H **39**
Blenheim Ho. PO14: Fare 4H **25**
Blenheim Rd. PO8: Horn 2A **10**
Bleriot Cres. PO15: White 4A **12**
Bliss Cl. PO7: W'lle 4G **19**
Blissford Cl. PO9: Hav 3H **21**
Blossom Dr. PO7: Wid 6E **19**
Blossom Sq. PO1: Ports 1C **4** (1A **50**)
Blount Rd. PO1: Ports 6D **4** (4B **50**)
Bluebell Cl. PO7: W'lle 3H **19**
Bluebell Way PO15: White 1A **12**
Blue Bldg. PO1: Ports 4C **4** (3A **50**)
Blueprint Portfield Rd. PO3: Ports 3C **42**
Blue Reef Aquarium
Southsea **6C 50**
The Boardwalk PO6: P Sol 4F **29**
The Boardwalk Shop. Cen. 5E **29**
BOARHUNT **4H 15**
Boarhunt Cl. PO1: Ports 2H **5** (2D **50**)
Boarhunt Rd. PO17: Boar, Fare 6E **15**
The Boatyard Ind. Est. PO16: Fare 3B **26**
Bodmin Rd. PO6: Cosh 3E **29**
Boiler Rd. PO1: Ports 6D **40**
Bolde Cl. PO3: Ports 2D **42**
Boldens Rd. PO12: Gos 6D **48**
Boldre Cl. PO9: Hav 5C **20**
Bolton Dr. PO12: Gos 6A **40**
The Boltons PO7: Purb 6G **19**
Bonchurch Rd. PO4: S'sea 2G **51**
Bondfields Cres. PO9: Hav 3E **21**
Bonfire Cnr. PO1: Ports 1B **4** (1A **50**)
Bordon Rd. PO9: Hav 4F **21**
The Borough *GU32: Pet 4C **56***
(off Borough Hill)
Borough Gro. GU32: Pet 5C **56**
Borough Hill GU32: Pet 4C **56**
Borough Rd. GU32: Pet 5B **56**
Bosham Rd. PO2: Ports 5B **42**
Bosham Wlk. PO13: Gos 3B **38**
Bosmere Gdns. PO10: Ems 2C **34**
Bosmere Rd. PO11: H Isl 5G **55**
Boston Cl. PO14: Titch 1A **24**
Boston Rd. PO6: Cosh 2A **30**
Bosuns Cl. PO16: Fare 5B **26**
Botley Dr. PO9: Hav 3D **20**
Boughton Ct. PO3: Ports 1E **43**
Boulter La. PO17: S'wick 2E **17**
Boulton Rd. PO5: S'sea 4E **51**
Boundary Wlk. PO17: K Vil 2G **13**
Boundary Way PO6: Cosh 1D **30**
PO9: Hav 2E **33**
Bound La. PO11: H Isl 5C **54**
Bourne Cl. PO8: Horn 1B **10**
Bournemouth Av. PO12: Gos 6G **39**
Bournemouth Ho. PO9: Hav 4G **21**
Bourne Rd. PO6: Cosh 3F **29**
Bourne Vw. Cl. PO10: S'brne 1H **35**
Bowen La. GU31: Pet 4D **56**
Bowers Cl. PO8: Cowp 3A **10**
Bowes Hill PO9: R Cas 4H **11**
Bowes-Lyon Ct. PO8: Horn 6B **6**
Bowler Av. PO3: Ports 1F **51**
Bowler Ct. PO3: Ports 1F **51**
Boxgrove Ho. PO1: Ports 1H **5** (1D **50**)
Boxwood Cl. PO7: W'lle 3G **19**
PO16: Portc 2H **27**
Boyd Buildilngs PO1: Ports 4B **4**
Boyd Cl. PO14: Stub 4D **36**
Boyd Rd. PO13: Gos 2B **38**
Boyes La. PO8: Blen, Ids 5F **7**
Boyle Ct. PO1: Ports 2E **51**
Boyle Cres. PO7: W'lle 4F **19**
Brabazon Rd. PO15: Seg 4A **12**
Bracken Cl. PO13: Lee S 1D **46**
Bracken Heath PO7: W'lle 6B **10**
Bracken Rd. GU31: Pet 5G **57**
Bracklesham Rd. PO11: H Isl 6H **55**
PO13: Gos 5D **38**
Bradford Ct. PO13: Gos 1G **47**
BRADFORD JUNC. **3E 51**
Bradford Rd. PO5: S'sea 4H **5** (3D **50**)
Brading Av. PO4: S'sea 5G **51**
PO13: Gos 3C **38**
Bradley Ct. PO9: Hav 3H **21**
Bradly Rd. PO15: Fare 1E **25**
Braemar Av. PO6: Cosh 4D **30**
Braemar Cl. PO13: Gos 3D **38**
PO15: Fare 6G **13**
Braemar Rd. PO13: Gos 2D **38**
Braganza Ho. PO1: Ports 5C **4**
Braintree Rd. PO6: Cosh 2H **29**
Braishfield Rd. PO9: Hav 5G **21**
Bramber Rd. PO12: Gos 6G **39**
Bramble Cl. PO9: Hav 6A **22**
PO14: Stub 4C **36**
Bramble Ct. *GU31: Pet 4G **57***
(off Rival Moor Rd.)
Bramble La. PO8: Clan 1F **7**
Bramble Rd. GU31: Pet 4G **57**
PO4: S'sea 3E **51**
The Brambles Bus. Cen. PO7: W'lle 1E **19**
Brambles Ent. Cen. PO7: W'lle 6E **9**
Brambles Farm Ind. Est. PO7: W'lle 1F **19**
Brambles Rd. PO13: Lee S 6F **37**
Bramble Way PO13: Gos 3A **38**
Brambling Rd. PO9: R Cas 6H **11**
Bramdean Dr. PO9: Hav 4D **20**
Bramham Moor PO14: Stub 3D **36**
Bramley Cl. PO7: W'lle 1H **19**
Bramley Gdns. PO10: S'brne 3F **35**
PO12: Gos 6C **48**
Bramley Ho. PO5: S'sea 5G **5** (3C **50**)
PO12: Gos 6D **48**
Brampton La. PO3: Ports 1E **43**
Bramshaw Ct. PO9: Hav 4H **21**
Bramshott Rd. PO4: S'sea 3F **51**
Brandon Ct. PO5: S'sea 4E **51**
Brandon Ho. PO5: S'sea 5E **51**
Brandon Rd. PO5: S'sea 5D **50**
Branewick Cl. PO15: Seg 6A **12**
Brankesmere Ter. *PO5: S'sea 4C **50***
(off Queen's Cres.)
Bransbury M. PO4: S'sea 4A **52**
Bransbury Rd. PO4: S'sea 4H **51**
Bransgore Av. PO9: Hav 5C **20**
Brasted Ct. PO4: S'sea 2A **52**
Braunston Cl. PO6: Cosh 2E **29**
Braxell Lawn PO9: Hav 3D **20**
BREACH **1H 35**
Breach Av. PO10: S'brne 1H **35**
Brecon Av. PO6: Dray 2D **30**
Brecon Cl. PO14: Fare 3G **25**
Brecon Ho. PO1: Ports 4B **4** (3A **50**)

A-Z Portsmouth 61

Bredenbury Cres.—Cams Alders Sports Cen.

Bredenbury Cres. PO6: Cosh 2G **29**
Bredon Wlk. PO14: Fare 3G **25**
Breech Cl. PO3: Ports 1B **42**
Brenchley Cl. PO16: Portc 4H **27**
Brendon Rd. PO14: Fare 3F **25**
Brent Ct. PO4: S'sea 2H **51**
PO10: Ems 3C **34**
Brent Ho. PO9: Hav 5D **20**
Bresler Ho. PO6: Cosh 2F **29**
Brewers La. PO13: Gos 3C **38**
Brewer St. PO1: Ports 1G **5** (1C **50**)
Brewster Cl. PO8: Cowp 4A **10**
Briar Cl. PO8: Horn 2B **10**
PO12: Gos 4A **48**
Briarfield Gdns. PO8: Horn 1B **10**
Briar Gdns. PO7: Purb 5G **19**
The Briars PO7: W'lle 1E **19**
Briarwood Cl. PO16: Fare 3B **26**
Briarwood Gdns. PO11: H Isl 4B **54**
Bridefield Cl. PO8: Cowp 4F **9**
Bridefield Cres. PO8: Cowp 4F **9**
Bridgefoot Dr. PO16: Fare 2C **26**
Bridgefoot Hill PO16: Fare 2D **26**
Bridgefoot Path PO10: Ems 3D **34**
Bridge Ho. PO13: Gos 1C **38**
Bridge Industries PO16: Fare 6C **14**
BRIDGEMARY 2C **38**
Bridgemary Av. PO13: Gos 2D **38**
Bridgemary Gro. PO13: Gos 1C **38**
Bridgemary Rd. PO13: Gos 6C **26**
Bridgemary Way PO13: Gos 6C **26**
Bridge Rd. PO10: Ems 2D **34**
Bridges Av. PO6: Cosh 2D **28**
The Bridge Shop. Cen. 2E **51**
Bridgeside Cl. PO1: Ports 2H **5** (2D **50**)
Bridge St. PO14: Titch 3C **24**
PO17: S'wick 3B **16**
PO17: Wick 1A **14**
Bridget Cl. PO8: Horn 6C **6**
Bridle Path PO8: Horn 5B **6**
Bridport Ho. *PO12: Gos* *6B* ***40***
(off Searle Dr.)
Bridport St. PO1: Ports 2G **5** (2C **50**)
Brigham Cl. PO2: Ports 2A **42**
Brighstone Rd. PO6: Cosh 4A **30**
Brighton Av. PO12: Gos 5F **39**
Brightside PO7: W'lle 3F **19**
Brights La. PO11: H Isl 2B **54**
Brisbane Ho. PO1: Ports 6H **41**
Bristol Ct. PO13: Gos 2G **47**
Bristol Rd. PO4: S'sea 5F **51**
Britain St. PO1: Ports 3C **4** (2A **50**)
Britannia Ho. *PO16: Fare* *2F* ***27***
(off Oysell Gdns.)
Britannia Rd. PO5: S'sea 3D **50**
Britannia Rd. Nth. PO5: S'sea 3D **50**
Britannia St. GU31: Pet 2E **57**
Britannia Way PO12: Gos 6A **40**
Britnell Ho. GU32: Pet 3D **56**
Britten Rd. PO13: Lee S 1C **46**
Britten Way PO7: W'lle 5G **19**
Brixworth Cl. PO6: Cosh 2E **29**
Broadacre Pl. PO14: Fare 3A **26**
Broadcut PO16: Fare 1C **26**
Broad Gdns. PO6: Farl 3G **31**
Broadlands Av. PO7: W'lle 3G **19**
Broadlaw Wlk. Shop. Cen. 4G **25**
Broadmarsh Bus. & Innovation Cen.
PO9: Hav 3C **32**
Broadmeadows La. PO7: W'lle 2A **20**
Broadmere Av. PO9: Hav 4F **21**
Broad Oak Bus. Pk. PO3: Ports 1D **42**
Broadsands Dr. PO12: Gos 4H **47**
Broadsands Wlk. PO12: Gos 4A **48**
Broad St. PO1: Ports 5A **4** (3H **49**)
Broad Wlk. PO8: Horn 2E **11**
PO9: R Cas 1E **23**
PO10: R Cas, Westb 2F **23**
Broadway La. PO8: Love 1F **9**
Broadway Pk. GU31: Pet 6D **56**
Brockenhurst Av. PO9: Hav 3D **20**
BROCKHAMPTON 2D **32**
Brockhampton La. PO9: Hav 2E **33**
Brockhampton Rd. PO9: Hav 3D **32**
(not continuous)
BROCKHURST 1C **48**
Brockhurst Ind. Est. PO12: Gos 4F **39**
Brockhurst Rd. PO12: Gos 5F **39**
Brocklands PO9: Hav 2D **32**
Brodrick Av. PO12: Gos 4C **48**
Brompton Pas. PO2: Ports 6H **41**
Brompton Rd. PO4: S'sea 5F **51**
Bromyard Cres. PO6: Cosh 2G **29**
Brookdale Cl. PO7: W'lle 1H **19**
Brooke Ho. PO9: Hav 1F **33**
Brookers La. PO13: Gos 2A **38**
(not continuous)
Brook Farm Av. PO15: Fare 1H **25**
Brookfield Cl. PO9: Hav 1E **33**
Brookfield Rd. PO1: Ports 1E **51**
Brook Gdns. PO10: Ems 3B **34**
Brooklands Ct. PO7: W'lle 6H **9**
Brooklands Rd. PO9: Bed 1B **32**
Brooklyn Dr. PO7: W'lle 1H **19**
Brookmeadow PO15: Fare 2H **25**
Brook Meadow Nature Reserve 2E **35**
Brookmead Way PO9: Langs 3F **33**
Brookside PO13: Gos 6B **26**
Brookside Cl. PO7: Den 3B **8**
Brookside Rd. PO9: Bed 1C **32**
PO9: Hav 3D **32**
Brooks Wlk. PO8: Clan 2H **7**
Brookview Cl. PO14: Fare 3D **24**
Broom Cl. PO4: S'sea 2B **52**
PO7: W'lle 4A **20**
Broomfield Cres. PO13: Gos 6B **38**
Broom Rd. GU31: Pet 5G **57**
Broom Sq. PO4: S'sea 2B **52**
Broom Way PO13: Lee S 6H **37**
Brougham La. PO12: Gos 1C **48**
Brougham Rd. PO5: S'sea 5F **5** (3C **50**)
Brougham St. PO12: Gos 1C **48**
The Brow PO7: Wid 1D **30**
PO12: Gos 3G **49**
Browndown Rd. PO12: Gos 4G **47**
PO13: Lee S 4G **47**
Brownfield Ho. GU32: Pet 3D **56**
Browning Av. PO6: Cosh 2C **28**
Brownlow Cl. PO1: Ports 6H **41**
Brownwich La. PO14: Titch 4A **24**
Brow Path PO7: Wid 1E **31**
Broxhead Rd. PO9: Hav 3G **21**
Bruce Cl. PO16: Fare 6A **14**
Bruce Rd. PO4: S'sea 5F **51**
Brune La. PO13: Lee S 4A **38**
(not continuous)
Brunel Ct. PO1: Ports 1D **50**
Brunel Rd. PO2: Ports 2A **42**
Brunel Way PO9: Bed 2B **32**
PO15: Seg 4A **12**
Brunswick PO1: Ports 2C **4**
Brunswick Gdns. PO9: Bed 1D **32**
Brunswick Pl. PO10: Ems 5D **22**
Brunswick St. PO5: S'sea 5F **5** (3C **50**)
Brushwood Gro. PO10: Ems 5D **22**
Bryher Bri. PO6: P Sol 4F **29**
Bryher Island PO6: P Sol 4E **29**
Bryony Way PO7: W'lle 2A **20**
Bryson Cl. PO13: Lee S 1E **47**
Bryson Rd. PO6: Cosh 3H **29**
Buckby La. PO3: Ports 1E **43**
Buckingham Ct. PO15: Fare 6F **13**
Buckingham Grn. PO1: Ports 6A **42**
Buckingham Pl. PO1: Ports 2G **5** (2C **50**)
Buckingham Rd. GU32: Pet 4B **56**
Buckingham St. PO1: Ports 1G **5** (1C **50**)
BUCKLAND 5H **41**
Buckland Cl. PO7: W'lle 4F **9**
Buckland Path PO2: Ports 6H **41**
Buckland St. PO2: Ports 6A **42**
(not continuous)
Bucklers Ct. PO2: Ports 4H **41**
PO9: Hav 2D **20**
Bucklers Rd. PO12: Gos 5A **40**
Buckmore Av. GU32: Pet 2B **56**
Bucksey Rd. PO13: Gos 5C **38**
Buddens Rd. PO17: Wick 1A **14**
Bude Cl. PO6: Cosh 2D **28**
Bulbarrow Wlk. PO14: Fare 3G **25**
Bulbeck Rd. PO9: Hav 2F **33**
Bullfinch Cl. PO10: Ems 5D **22**
Bullfinch Ct. PO13: Lee S 6H **37**
Bulls Copse La. PO8: Horn 1A **10**
Bulwark Rd. PO14: Stub 4D **36**
BUNKERS HILL 3A **8**
Bunkers Hill PO7: Den 4A **8**
Bunting Gdns. PO8: Cowp 3H **9**
Burbidge Gro. PO4: S'sea 5G **51**
Burcote Dr. PO3: Ports 1D **42**
Burdale Dr. PO11: H Isl 4F **55**
Burgate Cl. PO9: Bed 6D **20**
Burgesmede Ho. GU31: Pet 4D **56**
Burgess Cl. PO11: H Isl 6F **55**
Burghclere Rd. PO9: Hav 3H **21**
Burgoyne Rd. PO5: S'sea 6D **50**
Burgundy Ter. PO2: Ports 2A **42**
Buriton Cl. PO16: Portc 2B **28**
Buriton Ho. *PO1: Ports* *2H* ***5***
(off Buriton St.)
Buriton St. PO1: Ports 1H **5** (1D **50**)
Burleigh Rd. PO1: Ports 6B **42**
Burley Cl. PO9: Hav 3H **21**
Burlington Rd. PO2: Ports 4A **42**
Burnaby Rd. PO1: Ports 3D **4** (2B **50**)
Burnett Rd. PO12: Gos 1B **48**
Burney Ho. *PO12: Gos* *3F* ***49***
(off South St.)
Burney Rd. PO12: Gos 4A **48**
Burnham Rd. PO6: Dray 2F **31**
Burnham's Wlk. PO12: Gos 3F **49**
Burnham Wood PO16: Fare 6A **14**
Burnside PO7: W'lle 6A **10**
PO13: Gos 6B **26**
Burnt Ho. La. PO14: Stub 6F **25**
Burrell Ho. *PO5: S'sea* *4B* ***50***
(off Hambrook St.)
Burrfields Retail Pk. 4D **42**
Burrfields Rd. PO3: Ports 4C **42**
Burrill Av. PO6: Cosh 3C **30**
Burrows Cl. PO9: Hav 6G **21**
Bursledon Pl. PO7: Purb 4F **19**
Bursledon Rd. PO7: Purb 4F **19**
Burt Cl. PO15: Fare 6F **13**
Burwood Gro. PO11: H Isl 2C **54**
Bury Cl. PO12: Gos 3D **48**
Bury Cres. PO12: Gos 3D **48**
Bury Cross PO12: Gos 3C **48**
Bury Hall La. PO12: Gos 4A **48**
Bury Rd. PO12: Gos 3C **48**
Bush Ho. PO5: S'sea 6F **5** (4C **50**)
Bush St. E. PO5: S'sea 6F **5** (4C **50**)
Bush St. W. PO5: S'sea 6F **5** (4C **50**)
Bushy Mead PO7: Wid 6E **19**
Butcher St. PO1: Ports 3B **4** (2A **50**)
Butser Ct. PO8: Horn 2D **6**
Butser Wlk. GU31: Pet 3F **57**
PO14: Fare 3G **25**
Buttercup Way PO7: W'lle 5E **9**
Butterfly Dr. PO6: Cosh 2E **29**
Byerley Cl. PO10: Westb 4F **23**
Byerley Rd. PO1: Ports 2F **51**
(not continuous)
Byngs Bus. Pk. PO7: Den 5D **8**
Byrd Cl. PO7: W'lle 4G **19**
The Byres PO14: Stub 2E **37**
Byron Cl. PO16: Fare 1A **26**
Byron Rd. PO2: Ports 5B **42**

C

Cadgwith Pl. PO6: P Sol 4F **29**
Cadnam Ct. PO12: Gos 4H **47**
Cadnam Lawn PO9: Hav 2D **20**
Cadnam Rd. PO4: S'sea 4H **51**
Cador Dr. PO16: Portc 5H **27**
Caen Ho. PO14: Fare 3G **25**
Caer Peris Vw. PO16: Portc 1A **28**
Cains Cl. PO14: Stub 2E **37**
Cairo Ter. PO2: Ports 6H **41**
Caldecote Wlk. 4E **5** (3C **50**)
Calder Ho. PO1: Ports 2B **4**
Calgary Cl. PO7: Purb 5G **19**
Calshot Rd. PO9: Hav 2C **20**
Calshot Way PO13: Gos 4B **38**
Calthorpe Ho. PO12: Gos 6A **40**
Camaron Cvn. Pk. 5G **55**
Camber Ho. PO12: Gos 6B **40**
Camber Pl. PO1: Ports 6B **4** (4A **50**)
Cambrai Cl. PO3: Ports 6B **30**
Cambrian Ter. PO5: S'sea 6H **5**
Cambrian Wlk. PO14: Fare 4H **25**
CAMBRIDGE JUNC. 5D **4** (3B **50**)
Cambridge Rd. PO1: Ports 5D **4** (3B **50**)
PO12: Gos 1A **48**
PO13: Lee S 2D **46**
Camcross Cl. PO6: Cosh 2F **29**
Camden St. PO12: Gos 1C **48**
CAMDENTOWN 1C **48**
Camelia Cl. PO9: Hav 6A **22**
Camellia Way PO15: White 1A **12**
Camelot Cres. PO16: Portc 2H **27**
Cameron Cl. PO13: Gos 2C **38**
Campbell Cres. PO7: Purb 4E **19**
Campbell Mans. PO5: S'sea 4D **50**
Campbell Rd. PO5: S'sea 4D **50**
Campion Cl. PO7: W'lle 3A **20**
Camp Rd. PO13: Gos 2D **38**
Cams Alders Sports Cen. 4A **26**

Cooks La.—Dale Pk. Ho.

Cooks La. PO10: S'brne 2H **35**
PO18: S'brne 2H **35**
Cooley Ho. PO13: Gos 6B **26**
Coombe Farm Av. PO16: Fare 3A **26**
Coombe Rd. PO12: Gos 6H **39**
Coombs Cl. PO8: Horn 4C **6**
Cooperage Grn. PO12: Gos 2F **49**
Cooper Gro. PO16: Portc 5B **28**
Cooper Rd. PO3: Ports 5D **42**
COPNOR 4C **42**
Copnor Bri. Bus. Pk. PO3: Ports 6C **42**
Copnor Grn. PO3: Ports 6C **42**
Copnor Rd. PO3: Ports 6B **30**
Copper Beech Dr. PO6: Farl 3G **31**
Copperfield Ho. PO1: Ports 6H **41**
Copper St. PO5: S'sea 6E **5** (4B **50**)
The Coppice PO8: Horn 1A **10**
PO13: Gos 3D **38**
Coppice Way PO15: Fare 6F **13**
Coppins Gro. PO16: Portc 5A **28**
The Copse PO15: Fare 5F **13**
Copse Cl. GU31: Pet 3G **57**
PO7: Wid 1F **31**
Copse La. PO11: H Isl 5C **44**
PO13: Gos 4D **38**
Copsey Cl. PO6: Dray 3F **31**
Copsey Gro. PO6: Dray 4F **31**
Copsey Path PO6: Farl 3F **31**
Copythorn Rd. PO2: Ports 4B **42**
Coral Cl. PO16: Portc 5A **28**
Coral Ct. PO13: Gos 1G **47**
Coralin Gro. PO7: W'lle 6B **10**
Corbett Rd. PO7: W'lle 3F **19**
Corby Cres. PO3: Ports 1D **42**
Corfe Cl. PO14: Stub 3C **36**
Corhampton Cres. PO9: Hav 5D **20**
Corhampton Ho. PO1: Ports 1H **5**
Coriander Way PO15: White 1A **12**
Cormorant Cl. PO16: Portc 3F **27**
Cormorant Wlk. PO13: Gos 3B **38**
Cornaway La. PO16: Portc 4H **27**
Cornbrook Gro. PO7: W'lle 6C **10**
Cornelius Dr. PO7: W'lle 6A **10**
Corner Mead PO7: Den 3B **8**
Cornfield PO16: Fare 5B **14**
Cornfield Rd. PO13: Lee S 1D **46**
Cornflower Gdns. PO8: Clan 2H **7**
Cornwallis Cres. PO1: Ports 1D **50**
Cornwallis Ho. PO1: Ports 1H **5**
Cornwall Rd. PO1: Ports 2E **51**
Cornwell Cl. PO2: Ports 3F **41**
PO13: Gos 6D **38**
Coronado Rd. PO12: Gos 6H **39**
Coronation Homes PO2: Ports 1A **42**
Coronation Rd. PO7: W'lle 1G **19**
PO11: H Isl 6G **55**
Corsair Cl. PO13: Lee S 2E **47**
Corsham Ho. *PO15: Seg 6B 12*
(off Park Cott. Dr.)
Cort Way PO15: Fare 5E **13**
COSHAM 5B **30**
Cosham Pk. Av. PO6: Cosh 4B **30**
Cosham Station (Rail) 4B **30**
Cotswold Cl. PO9: Hav 3E **21**
Cotswold Ho. PO6: Cosh 3G **29**
Cotswold Wlk. PO14: Fare 4H **25**
Cotswold Way PO7: W'lle 6E **9**
Cottage Cl. PO7: Den 4B **8**
Cottage Gro. PO5: S'sea 5G **5** (3C **50**)
PO12: Gos 2D **48**
Cottage Vw. PO1: Ports 2H **5** (2D **50**)
Cotteridge Ho. PO5: S'sea 4H **5** (2D **50**)
Cottesloe Ct. PO5: S'sea 5C **50**
Cottes Way PO14: Stub 4C **36**
Cottes Way East PO14: Stub 4D **36**
Cotton Dr. PO10: Ems 5C **22**
(not continuous)
Cotton Rd. PO3: Ports 1G **51**
Cottonwood Cl. PO7: Purb 4E **19**
Cotwell Av. PO8: Cowp 3B **10**
Coulmere Rd. PO12: Gos 1C **48**
Coulter Rd. PO7: W'lle 6E **9**
Country Vw. PO14: Stub 1D **36**
County Gdns. PO14: Fare 3E **25**
Court Barn Cl. PO13: Lee S 6H **37**
Court Barn La. PO13: Lee S 6H **37**
Court Cl. PO6: Cosh 4D **30**
Courtenay Cl. PO15: Seg 6A **12**
Courtlands Ter. PO8: Cowp 3A **10**
Court La. PO6: Cosh 4D **30**
Court Mead PO6: Cosh 3D **30**
Courtmount Gro. PO6: Cosh 3C **30**
Courtmount Path PO6: Cosh 2C **30**
Court Rd. PO13: Lee S 6G **37**
The Courtyard GU31: Pet 4D **56**
Cousins Gro. PO4: S'sea 5G **51**
Coverack Way PO6: P Sol 4F **29**
Covert Gro. PO7: W'lle 4A **20**
Covindale Ho. PO4: S'sea 4G **51**
Covington Rd. PO10: Westb 4F **23**
Cowan Rd. PO7: W'lle 4F **19**
Coward Rd. PO12: Gos 5B **48**
Cowdray Ho. PO1: Ports 2H **5**
Cowdray Pk. PO14: Stub 3C **36**
Cowes Ct. PO14: Fare 3E **25**
Cow La. PO6: Cosh 4H **29**
PO16: Portc 4B **28**
Cowper Rd. PO1: Ports 1E **51**
COWPLAIN 4A **10**
Cowplain Activity Cen. 4B **10**
Cowslip Cl. PO13: Gos 3C **38**
Cowslip Ct. PO7: W'lle 5E **9**
Cowslip Gro. PO8: Clan 2H **7**
Coxes Mdw. GU32: Pet 2C **56**
Crabbe Ct. PO5: S'sea 5G **5** (3C **50**)
Crabden La. PO8: Blen 5E **7**
CRABTHORN 2D **36**
Crabthorn Farm La. PO14: Stub 2D **36**
Crabwood Ct. PO9: Hav 2D **20**
Craddock Ho. PO1: Ports 2B **4**
Crafts La. GU31: Pet 2E **57**
Craigbank Ct. PO14: Fare 2H **25**
Craig Ho. *PO5: S'sea 5D 50*
(off Marmion Av.)
Craigwell Rd. PO7: Purb 5G **19**
Cranborne Rd. PO6: Cosh 2C **30**
Cranborne Wlk. PO14: Fare 4G **25**
Cranbourne Rd. PO12: Gos 4E **49**
Crane Cl. PO13: Gos 3B **38**
Crane Ct. *PO4: S'sea 2H 51*
(off Velder Av.)
Cranesbill Ct. PO10: Ems 5E **23**
Craneswater Av. PO4: S'sea 6E **51**
Craneswater Ga. PO4: S'sea 6E **51**
Craneswater M. *PO4: S'sea 5E 51*
(off Craneswater Pk.)
Craneswater Pk. PO4: S'sea 5E **51**
Cranford Rd. GU32: Pet 5B **56**
Cranleigh Av. PO1: Ports 1E **51**
Cranleigh Rd. PO1: Ports 1E **51**
PO16: Portc 4G **27**
Crasswell St. PO1: Ports 1G **5** (1C **50**)
(not continuous)
Craven Ct. PO15: Fare 6G **13**
Crawford Dr. PO16: Fare 6H **13**
Crawley Av. PO9: Hav 3G **21**
Crawters La. *GU31: Pet 4D 56*
(off College St.)
Cray Ho. PO12: Gos 3E **49**
Credenhill Rd. PO6: Cosh 2G **29**
Creech Vw. PO7: Den 3A **8**
Creek End PO10: Ems 4D **34**
Creek Rd. PO11: H Isl 5F **55**
PO12: Gos 3F **49**
Cremer Mall PO16: Fare 2B **26**
Cremorne Pl. GU32: Pet 3D **56**
Cremyll Cl. PO14: Stub 3E **37**
The Crescent PO1: Ports 4C **4** (3A **50**)
PO7: Purb 5E **19**
PO10: S'brne 3H **35**
Crescent Gdns. PO16: Fare 2A **26**
Crescent Rd. PO12: Gos 6C **48**
PO16: Fare 2A **26**
Cressy Rd. PO2: Ports 6H **41**
The Crest PO7: Wid 1E **31**
Cresta Ct. PO4: S'sea 5F **51**
Crest Cl. PO16: Fare 2D **26**
Crestland Cl. PO8: Cowp 4A **10**
Cricket Dr. PO8: Cowp 2A **10**
Cricketers Way PO9: Hav 5E **21**
Crinoline Gdns. PO4: S'sea 5G **51**
Crisspyn Cl. PO8: Horn 1B **10**
Croad Ct. PO16: Fare 2C **26**
Crockford Dr. GU31: Pet 6C **56**
Crockford Rd. PO10: Westb 5F **23**
The Croft PO14: Stub 1E **37**
Croftlands Av. PO14: Stub 2E **37**
Croft La. PO11: H Isl 4C **44**
Crofton Av. PO13: Lee S 5E **37**
Crofton Cl. PO7: Purb 4E **19**
Crofton Ct. PO14: Stub 3E **37**
Crofton La. PO14: Stub 4D **36**
Crofton Rd. PO2: Ports 3A **42**
PO4: S'sea 2H **51**
Croft Rd. PO2: Ports 4H **41**
Cromarty Av. PO4: S'sea 3H **51**
Cromarty Cl. PO14: Stub 2D **36**
Crombie Cl. PO8: Cowp 3H **9**
Cromer Rd. PO6: Cosh 2A **30**
Cromhall Cl. PO14: Fare 3E **25**
Cromwell Rd. PO4: S'sea 5H **51**
Crondall Av. PO9: Hav 3E **21**
Crooked Wlk. La. PO17: S'wick 6C **16**
Crookham Cl. PO9: Hav 4C **20**
CROOKHORN 6G **19**
Crookhorn La. PO7: Purb 2G **31**
Crossbill Cl. PO8: Horn 6A **6**
Crossfell Wlk. PO14: Fare 4G **25**
Crossland Cl. PO12: Gos 4E **49**
Crossland Dr. PO9: Hav 6F **21**
Cross La. PO8: Horn 2A **10**
Cross Rd. PO13: Lee S 3E **47**
Cross St. PO1: Ports 2C **4** (2A **50**)
PO5: S'sea 4H **5** (3D **50**)
Cross Way PO9: Hav 1E **33**
The Crossway PO16: Portc 3H **27**
The Crossways PO12: Gos 1D **48**
Crouch La. PO8: Horn 6A **6**
Crown Bingo 4F **21**
Crown Cl. PO7: Purb 6G **19**
Crown Ct. PO1: Ports 1D **50**
(Crown St.)
PO1: Ports 6C **4**
(Peacock La.)
Crown M. PO12: Gos 3F **49**
Crown St. PO1: Ports 1D **50**
Crowsbury Cl. PO10: Ems 6C **22**
Croxton Rd. PO5: S'sea 6D **4** (4B **50**)
Crundles GU31: Pet 4E **57**
Crusader Ct. PO12: Gos 6A **40**
Crystal Way PO7: W'lle 1A **20**
Cuckoo Cl. PO10: Ems 6E **23**
Cuckoo La. PO14: Stub 2D **36**
Culdrose Ho. PO13: Gos 2H **47**
Culloden Cl. PO15: Fare 1G **25**
Culloden Rd. PO14: Fare 5H **25**
Culver Dr. PO11: H Isl 6E **55**
Culverin Sq. PO3: Ports 1C **42**
Culver Rd. PO4: S'sea 5G **51**
Cumberland Av. PO10: Ems 5C **22**
Cumberland Bus. Cen. PO5: S'sea 2D **50**
Cumberland Ct. PO4: S'sea 5F **51**
Cumberland Ho. PO1: Ports 1C **4** (1A **50**)
PO13: Gos 2G **47**
Cumberland House Natural History Mus. 6F **51**
Cumberland Rd. PO5: S'sea 2D **50**
Cumberland St. PO1: Ports 1C **4** (1A **50**)
Cumberland Way PO7: W'lle 6E **9**
Cunningham Av. PO2: Ports 1A **42**
Cunningham Cl. PO2: Ports 1H **41**
Cunningham Ct. *PO5: S'sea 5D 50*
(off Collingwood Rd.)
Cunningham Dr. PO13: Gos 2D **38**
Cunningham Rd. PO7: W'lle 4F **19**
PO8: Horn 6C **6**
Curdridge Cl. PO9: Hav 4G **21**
Curie Rd. PO6: Cosh 2B **30**
Curlew Cl. PO10: Ems 3C **34**
Curlew Dr. PO16: Portc 3F **27**
Curlew Gdns. PO8: Cowp 3H **9**
Curlew Path PO4: S'sea 2H **51**
Curlew Wlk. PO13: Gos 2A **38**
Curtis Mead PO2: Ports 1B **42**
Curtiss Gdns. PO12: Gos 3B **48**
The Curve PO8: Love 1H **9**
PO13: Gos 2B **38**
Curzon Howe Rd. PO1: Ports 2C **4** (2A **50**)
Cuthbert Rd. PO1: Ports 1F **51**
Cutlers La. PO14: Stub 2E **37**
Cydney Ter. *PO1: Ports 2E 51*
(off Sandringham Rd.)
Cygnet Ct. PO16: Portc 3F **27**
Cygnet Ho. PO12: Gos 6H **39**
Cygnet Rd. PO6: Farl 4H **31**
Cypress Cres. PO8: Horn 2A **10**
Cyprus Rd. PO2: Ports 5A **42**

D

Daffodil Way PO9: Hav 1A **34**
Dairymoor PO17: Wick 1A **14**
Daisy La. PO12: Gos 3C **48**
Daisy Mead PO7: W'lle 3A **20**
Dakota Bus. Pk. PO9: Hav 5H **21**
The Dale PO7: Wid 1E **31**
Dale Dr. PO13: Gos 6B **26**
Dale Pk. Ho. PO1: Ports 2G **5** (2C **50**)

Dale Rd.—Dunsmore Cl.

Dale Rd. PO14: Stub 2F **37**
Dale Sq. PO9: Hav 3C **20**
Dalewood Rd. PO15: Fare 2F **25**
Dallington Cl. PO14: Stub 4E **37**
Damask Gdns. PO7: W'lle 6B **10**
Dame Elizabeth Kelly Ct. *PO2: Ports 1A 42*
(off Phoenix Sq.)
Dame Judith Way PO6: Cosh 3B **30**
Dampier Cl. PO13: Gos 6C **38**
Danbury Ct. PO10: Ems 1E **35**
Dances Way PO11: H Isl 3A **54**
Dandelion Cl. PO13: Gos 3B **38**
Dando Rd. PO7: Den 3C **8**
Danebury Cl. PO9: Hav 3E **21**
Danesbrook La. PO7: W'lle 2A **20**
Danes Rd. PO16: Portc 1H **27**
Daniels Cl. PO12: Gos 3A **48**
Dark Hollow GU32: Pet 3C **56**
Darlington Rd. PO4: S'sea 4E **51**
Darnel Cres. PO7: W'lle 5E **9**
Darnel Rd. PO7: W'lle 6D **8**
Darnley La. PO7: W'lle 1E **19**
Darren Cl. PO14: Stub 1F **37**
Darren Ct. PO16: Fare 1B **26**
Dartmouth Cl. PO12: Gos 6A **40**
Dartmouth Ct. *PO12: Gos 6A 40*
(off Dartmouth Cl.)
Dartmouth M. PO5: S'sea 6E **5** (4B **50**)
Dartmouth Rd. PO3: Ports 3C **42**
Darwin Cl. PO13: Lee S 6H **37**
Darwin Ho. PO1: Ports 2H **5**
Daubney Gdns. PO9: Hav 3D **20**
Daulston Rd. PO1: Ports 6B **42**
Davenport Cl. PO13: Gos 1G **47**
Daventry La. PO3: Ports 1E **43**
David Harmer Ho. *PO1: Ports 2D 50*
(off Arundel St.)
Davidia Ct. PO7: W'lle 3A **20**
David Lloyd Leisure
Port Solent 5F **29**
David Newberry Dr. PO13: Lee S 1E **47**
Davis Cl. PO13: Gos 5C **38**
Davis Way PO14: Fare 5A **26**
Daw La. PO11: H Isl 5B **44**
Dayshes Cl. PO13: Gos 2B **38**
Dayslondon Rd. PO7: Purb 4F **19**
D-Day Mus. & Overlord Embroidery 6C **50**
Deal Cl. PO14: Stub 1E **37**
Deal Rd. PO6: Cosh 2A **30**
Deane Ct. PO9: Hav 4H **21**
Deane Gdns. PO13: Lee S 1D **46**
Deane's Pk. Rd. PO16: Fare 2D **26**
Dean Farm Est. PO17: Fare 4A **14**
Dean Rd. PO6: Cosh 3C **30**
Deans Ga. PO14: Stub 4E **37**
Dean St. PO1: Ports 3C **4** (2A **50**)
Deanswood Dr. PO7: W'lle 6G **9**
Dean Vs. PO17: K Vil 3G **13**
Debney Lodge PO7: W'lle 2H **19**
Deep Dell PO8: Horn 2B **10**
Deeping Ga. PO7: W'lle 2A **20**
Deergrass Wlk. PO17: K Vil 2F **13**
Deerhurst Cres. PO6: Cosh 2E **29**
Deer Leap PO15: F'ley 4F **13**
Delamere Rd. PO4: S'sea 4E **51**
Delft Gdns. PO8: Cowp 5F **9**
De Lisle Cl. PO2: Ports 1B **42**
Delius Wlk. PO7: W'lle 4G **19**
The Dell PO9: Bed 1B **32**
PO16: Fare 2D **26**
Dell Cl. PO7: Wid 1D **30**
Dellcrest Path PO6: Cosh 2D **30**
(not continuous)
PO7: Wid 1D **30**
Dellfield Cl. PO6: Cosh 2E **29**
Dell Piece E. PO8: Horn 2D **10**
Dell Piece W. PO8: Horn 1B **10**
Dell Quay Cl. PO13: Gos 3B **38**
Delme Ct. PO16: Fare 2A **26**
Delme Dr. PO16: Fare 1D **26**
Delme Sq. PO16: Fare 2B **26**
Delphi Way PO7: Purb 1H **31**
Delta Bus. Pk. PO16: Fare 4B **26**
Denbigh Dr. PO16: Fare 1H **25**
Dene Ct. PO8: Cowp 5A **10**
Dene Hollow PO6: Dray 3F **31**
Denham Cl. PO14: Stub 3D **36**
Denhill Cl. PO11: H Isl 2A **54**
DENMEAD 2B **8**
Denmead Ho. PO1: Ports 1H **5** (1D **50**)
Denmead La. PO7: Den 1D **8**
Denmead Pk. PO7: Den 3C **8**
Denn Flds. PO9: Hav 1G **33**
Denning M. PO5: S'sea 3G **5** (2C **50**)
Dennistone Dene PO7: W'lle 2F **19**
Denville Av. PO16: Portc 5B **28**
Denville Cl. PO6: Farl 3H **31**
Denville Cl. Path PO6: Farl 3H **31**
DENVILLES 1H **33**
Denvilles Cl. PO9: Hav 1H **33**
Derby Ct. PO13: Gos 1G **47**
Derby Rd. PO2: Ports 4H **41**
Derlyn Rd. PO16: Fare 2A **26**
Dersingham Cl. PO6: Cosh 2A **30**
Derwent Cl. PO8: Horn 3C **6**
PO14: Stub 1F **37**
Derwent Rd. PO13: Lee S 2D **46**
Desborough Cl. PO6: Cosh 2E **29**
Deverell Pl. PO7: Wid 6E **19**
Devon La. PO7: W'lle 6E **9**
Devon Rd. PO3: Ports 2C **42**
Devonshire Av. PO4: S'sea 3F **51**
Devonshire Sq. PO4: S'sea 3F **51**
Devonshire Way PO14: Fare 3E **25**
Dewberry Gro. PO8: Clan 2H **7**
Dexter Dr. PO7: W'lle 6E **9**
Dhekelia Ct. PO1: Ports 1D **50**
Diamond St. PO5: S'sea 6E **5** (4B **50**)
Diana Cl. PO10: Ems 5C **22**
PO12: Gos 3A **48**
Dibber Rd. PO7: W'lle 6E **9**
Dibden Cl. PO9: Hav 5C **20**
Dickens Cl. PO2: Ports 6H **41**
Dickens Ho. PO4: S'sea 3H **51**
Dickins La. GU31: Pet 2E **57**
Dickinson Rd. PO4: S'sea 2F **51**
Dickson Pk. PO17: Wick 1A **14**
Dieppe Cres. PO2: Ports 1A **42**
Dieppe Gdns. PO12: Gos 3B **48**
Dight Rd. PO12: Gos 5E **49**
Dilkusha Ct. PO11: H Isl 5C **54**
Discovery Cl. PO14: Stub 6E **25**
Ditch Acre Gro. PO8: Clan 1D **6**
Ditcham Cres. PO9: Hav 5E **21**
Ditton Cl. PO14: Stub 2E **37**
The Diving Museum 5H **47**
Dockenfield Cl. PO9: Hav 5C **20**
Dock Mill Cotts. PO5: S'sea 5D **50**
Dock Rd. PO12: Gos 3E **49**
Dogwood Dell PO7: W'lle 4H **19**
Dolman Rd. PO12: Gos 4E **49**
Dolphin Ct. PO4: S'sea 6F **51**
PO13: Lee S 1C **46**
PO14: Stub 1D **36**
Dolphin Cres. PO12: Gos 4E **49**
Dolphin Quay PO10: Ems 3E **35**
Dolphin Way PO12: Gos 6F **49**
Dombey Ct. *PO1: Ports 6H 41*
(off Victoria St.)
Dominie Wlk. PO13: Lee S 1D **46**
Domum Rd. PO2: Ports 3B **42**
Domvilles App. PO2: Ports 4F **41**
Donaldson Rd. PO6: Cosh 5B **30**
Donnelly St. PO12: Gos 1C **48**
Don Styler Physical Training Cen. 3G **39**
Dorcas Cl. PO7: W'lle 6A **10**
Dore Av. PO16: Portc 3H **27**
Doric Cl. PO10: S'brne 2H **35**
Dorking Cres. PO6: Cosh 4B **30**
Dormington Rd. PO6: Cosh 2G **29**
Dormy Way PO13: Gos 4B **38**
Dorney Ct. PO6: Cosh 4C **30**
Dornmere La. PO7: W'lle 2A **20**
Dorothy Ct. PO5: S'sea 4D **50**
Dorothy Dymond St. PO1: Ports 3F **5** (2C **50**)
Dorrien Rd. PO12: Gos 6H **39**
Dorrita Av. PO8: Cowp 3A **10**
Dorrita Cl. PO4: S'sea 5F **51**
Dorset Cl. PO8: Horn 1B **10**
Dorstone Rd. PO6: Cosh 2G **29**
Douglas Gdns. PO9: Hav 5G **21**
Douglas Rd. PO3: Ports 6C **42**
Dove Cl. PO8: Cowp 3H **9**
Dover Cl. PO14: Stub 2D **36**
Dover Ct. PO11: H Isl 2A **54**
Dovercourt Rd. PO6: Cosh 5C **30**
Dover Rd. PO3: Ports 5C **42**
Dowley Ct. PO14: Titch 3B **24**
DOWNEND 2E **27**
Down End PO6: Dray 2E **31**
Down End Rd. PO6: Dray 2E **31**
PO16: Fare 2F **27**
PO17: Fare 2F **27**
Down Farm Pl. PO8: Horn 4C **6**
Downham Cl. PO8: Cowp 4H **9**
Downhouse Rd. PO8: Cath, Clan 1A **6**
Downley Point PO9: Hav 5H **21**
Downley Rd. PO9: Hav 6H **21**
Down Rd. PO8: Horn 4B **6**
Downs Cl. PO7: Purb 6H **19**
Downside PO13: Gos 3D **38**
Downside Rd. PO7: Wid 6E **19**
The Downsway PO16: Portc 3A **28**
Downton Ho. PO6: Cosh 2G **29**
Down Vw. Way PO8: Clan 1H **7**
Downwood Way PO8: Horn 4C **6**
Doyle Av. PO2: Ports 1A **42**
Doyle Cl. PO2: Ports 1A **42**
PO9: Hav 2D **32**
Doyle Ct. PO2: Ports 2A **42**
Doyle Ho. PO9: Bed 6B **20**
Dragon Est. PO6: Farl 4G **31**
Dragon St. GU31: Pet 4D **56**
Dragoon Ho. PO7: W'lle 6E **9**
Drake Ho. PO1: Ports 2B **4** (2A **50**)
Drake Rd. PO13: Lee S 6F **37**
Draycote Rd. PO8: Cath 2C **6**
DRAYTON 4E **31**
Drayton Ct. PO6: Farl 3F **31**
Drayton La. PO6: Dray 2D **30**
(not continuous)
Drayton Park 5D **30**
Drayton Rd. PO2: Ports 4A **42**
Dreadnought Ho. PO12: Gos 6A **40**
Dreadnought Rd. PO14: Fare 6H **25**
Dresden Dr. PO8: Cowp 4F **9**
The Drift PO9: R Cas 6H **11**
Drift Rd. PO8: Clan 2F **7**
PO16: Fare 1D **26**
Driftwood Dr. PO14: Fare 3F **25**
Driftwood Gdns. PO4: S'sea 5A **52**
Drill Shed Rd. PO2: Ports 4F **41**
The Drive PO9: Hav 6F **21**
PO10: S'brne 3H **35**
PO13: Gos 3A **38**
PO16: Fare 2A **26**
The Driveway PO4: S'sea 2A **52**
The Droke PO6: Cosh 4B **30**
(not continuous)
Drove Rd. PO17: S'wick 5E **17**
Droxford Cl. PO12: Gos 3B **48**
Droxford Rd. PO17: Wick 1B **14**
Drum La. GU32: Pet 3D **56**
Drum Mead GU32: Pet 4C **56**
Drummond Rd. PO1: Ports 1H **5** (1D **50**)
PO15: Seg 5A **12**
Dryden Av. PO6: Cosh 2C **28**
Dryden Cl. PO7: W'lle 5G **9**
PO16: Fare 1H **25**
Drysdale M. PO4: S'sea 5H **51**
Duckpond La. PO8: Blen 5E **7**
Duck Stile La. PO8: Blen 5E **7**
Duckworth Ho. PO1: Ports 3C **4** (2A **50**)
Dudleston Heath Dr. PO8: Cowp 5B **10**
Dudley Rd. PO3: Ports 6C **42**
Duffield La. PO10: W'cote 6H **23**
Dugald Drummond St.
PO1: Ports 3F **5** (2C **50**)
Duisburg Way PO5: S'sea 4B **50**
Duke Cres. PO1: Ports 6H **41**
Duke of Edinburgh Ho. PO1: Ports 1D **4**
Dukes Cl. GU32: Pet 3B **56**
PO10: Westb 6F **23**
Dukes Rd. PO12: Gos 1C **48**
Dukes Wlk. PO7: W'lle 2G **19**
Dukes Wlk. Service Rd. PO7: W'lle 2G **19**
Duke Ter. PO9: Hav 5D **20**
Dumbarton Cl. PO2: Ports 5H **41**
Dummer Ct. PO9: Hav 3D **20**
Dunbar Rd. PO4: S'sea 3H **51**
Duncan Cooper Ho. PO7: W'lle 2F **19**
Duncan Rd. PO5: S'sea 5D **50**
Duncans Dr. PO14: Fare 3D **24**
Duncton Rd. PO8: Clan 2H **7**
Duncton Way PO13: Gos 2C **38**
Dundas Cl. PO3: Ports 3D **42**
Dundas La. PO3: Ports 4D **42**
Dundas Spur PO3: Ports 3D **42**
Dundee Cl. PO15: Fare 6G **13**
Dundonald Cl. PO11: H Isl 2C **54**
Dunhurst Cl. PO9: Hav 6G **21**
Dunkeld Rd. PO12: Gos 6F **39**
Dunlin Cl. PO4: S'sea 2B **52**
PO10: Ems 5E **23**
Dunn Cl. PO4: S'sea 4H **51**
Dunnock Cl. PO9: R Cas 6H **11**
DUNSBURY PARK 2B **20**
Dunsbury Way PO9: Hav 3E **21**
Dunsmore Cl. PO5: S'sea 5F **5** (3C **50**)

66 A-Z Portsmouth

Golden Ct.—Hangers West

Golden Ct. PO7: W'lle 2G **19**
Goldfinch La. PO13: Lee S 6H **37**
Goldring Cl. PO11: H Isl 4C **54**
Goldsmith Av. PO4: S'sea 3E **51**
Gold St. PO5: S'sea 6E **5** (4B **50**)
Gomer Ct. PO12: Gos 4A **48**
Gomer La. PO12: Gos 3A **48**
Goodman Ct. PO1: Ports 5E **5**
Goodsell Cl. PO14: Stub 3D **36**
Goodwood Cl. PO8: Cowp 6B **10**
PO12: Gos 5H **39**
Goodwood Ct. PO10: S'brne 3H **35**
Goodwood Rd. PO5: S'sea 4E **51**
PO12: Gos 5H **39**
Goodyer Cl. GU32: Pet 5C **56**
Goose Grn. Cvn. Pk. 5G **55**
Gordon Rd. PO1: Ports 4B **50**
PO7: W'lle 3F **19**
PO10: S'brne 4F **35**
PO12: Gos 3C **48**
PO16: Fare 2A **26**
Goring Av. PO8: Clan 2H **7**
Gorley Ct. PO9: Hav 3D **20**
Gorran Av. PO13: Gos 4C **38**
Gorron Ho. PO11: H Isl 5A **54**
Gorselands Way PO13: Gos 5D **38**
Gorse Rd. GU31: Pet 4G **57**
The Gorseway PO11: H Isl 4H **53**
GOSPORT 3F **49**
Gosport & District Angling Club 6C **48**
Gosport & Stokes Bay Golf Course 6E **49**
Gosport Borough FC 3B **48**
Gosport Bus. Cen. PO13: Gos 3E **39**
Gosport Bus Station 3G **49**
Gosport Gallery 3F **49**
Gosport Ho. PO9: Hav 4H **21**
Gosport Rd. PO13: Lee S 2D **46**
PO14: Stub 2F **37**
PO16: Fare 4B **26**
Gosport Shop. Precinct 3F **49**
GOSPORT WAR MEMORIAL HOSPITAL 3C **48**
GOSPORT WAR MEMORIAL HOSPITAL MIU 3C **48**
Gothic Bldgs. PO5: S'sea 6H **5** (4D **50**)
Goyda Ho. PO12: Gos 1B **48**
Gracefields PO14: Fare 3D **24**
Grace Gdns. PO9: Hav 5E **21**
Graduate Ct. PO6: Cosh 5C **30**
Grafton Cl. PO12: Gos 6A **40**
Grafton St. PO2: Ports 6G **41**
Graham Rd. PO4: S'sea 4E **51**
PO12: Gos 1C **48**
Grainger St. PO7: W'lle 2E **19**
Granada Cl. PO8: Cowp 4A **10**
Granada Rd. PO4: S'sea 6E **51**
The Granary & Bakery PO12: Gos 1F **49**
Grand Division Row PO4: S'sea 4H **51**
Grand Pde. PO1: Ports 6B **4** (4A **50**)
PO11: H Isl 5C **54**
GRANGE 1H **47**
The Grange *PO10: Ems* *1D* ***34***
(off New Brighton Rd.)
Grange Cl. PO9: Hav 1H **33**
PO12: Gos 1B **48**
Grange Cres. PO12: Gos 1B **48**
Grange La. PO13: Gos 5C **38**
(not continuous)
Grange Rd. GU32: Pet 5C **56**
PO2: Ports 4H **41**
PO13: Gos 3H **47**
Grant Rd. PO6: Farl 3F **31**
Granville Cl. PO9: Warb 2G **33**
Grasmere Ho. PO6: Cosh 2F **29**
Grasmere Way PO14: Stub 1F **37**
Grassmere Way PO7: W'lle 6B **10**
Grateley Cres. PO9: Hav 5C **20**
Grayland Cl. PO11: H Isl 3A **54**
Grays Cl. PO12: Gos 4A **48**
Grays Ct. PO1: Ports 5C **4** (3A **50**)
Grayshott Rd. PO4: S'sea 3F **51**
PO12: Gos 3B **48**
Grayson Cl. PO13: Lee S 1E **47**
Gt. Copse Dr. PO9: Hav 3E **21**
Greater Horseshoe Way
PO17: K Vil 1G **13**
Greatfield Way PO9: R Cas 4H **11**
Great Gays PO14: Stub 4C **36**
Great Hanger GU31: Pet 4F **57**
Great Mead PO7: Den 4C **8**
GREAT POSBROOK 4B **24**
Great Salterns Golf Course 4D **42**
Gt. Southsea St. PO5: S'sea 6F **5** (4C **50**)
Grebe Cl. PO8: Cowp 3G **9**
PO10: Westb 5F **23**
PO16: Portc 3F **27**
The Green PO7: Den 2A **8**
PO9: R Cas 5H **11**
Greenacre Gdns. PO7: Purb 5F **19**
Greenbanks Gdns. PO16: Fare 1D **26**
Green Cres. PO13: Gos 4C **38**
The Greendale PO15: Fare 5F **13**
Greendale Cl. PO15: Fare 5F **13**
Green Farm Gdns. PO3: Ports 1B **42**
Greenfield Cres. PO8: Cowp 4B **10**
PO8: Horn 2C **10**
Greenfield Ri. PO8: Cowp 4B **10**
Greenhaven Cvn. Pk. 6G **55**
Green Haven Ct. PO8: Cowp 4A **10**
Grn. Hollow Cl. PO16: Fare 5H **13**
Green La. PO3: Ports 2B **42**
PO7: Den 2A **8**
PO8: Clan 1C **6**
PO11: H Isl 4A **54**
PO12: Gos 5A **40**
(Bucklers Rd.)
PO12: Gos 5C **48**
(Little Green)
Greenlea Cl. PO7: Wid 1D **30**
Greenlea Gro. PO12: Gos 6F **39**
Green Link PO13: Lee S 2D **46**
Grn. Pond Cnr. PO9: Warb 2H **33**
Green Rd. PO5: S'sea 6F **5** (4C **50**)
PO12: Gos 5C **48**
PO14: Stub 1E **37**
Green Wlk. PO15: Fare 6G **13**
The Greenway PO10: Ems 6D **22**
Greenway Rd. PO12: Gos 1D **48**
Greenwich Ct. PO5: S'sea 5F **5**
Greenwood Av. PO6: Cosh 3H **29**
Greenwood Cl. PO16: Fare 5A **14**
Greetham St. PO5: S'sea 3G **5** (2C **50**)
Gregson Av. PO13: Gos 2C **38**
Gregson Cl. PO13: Gos 2C **38**
Grenehurst Way GU31: Pet 4D **56**
Grenfield Ct. PO10: Ems 6D **22**
Grenville Ho. PO1: Ports 3C **4**
Grenville Rd. PO4: S'sea 4E **51**
Grevillea Av. PO15: Seg 6A **12**
Greville Grn. PO10: Ems 5C **22**
Greyfriars Ct. PO5: S'sea 4C **50**
Greyfriars Rd. PO15: Fare 1E **25**
Greyshott Av. PO14: Fare 3E **25**
Greywell Hgts. *PO9: Hav* *5E* ***21***
(off Dunsbury Way)
Greywell Rd. PO9: Hav 4F **21**
Greywell Shop. Cen. 4F **21**
Greywell Sq. PO9: Hav 4F **21**
Griffin Wlk. PO13: Gos 1G **47**
Grindle Cl. PO16: Portc 2A **28**
Gritanwood Rd. PO4: S'sea 4H **51**
Grosvenor Ct. *PO9: Hav* *2F* ***33***
(off East St.)
PO14: Stub 3F **37**
Grosvenor Ho. PO5: S'sea 5G **5** (3C **50**)
Grosvenor M. PO12: Gos 2E **49**
Grosvenor St. PO5: S'sea 4G **5** (3C **50**)
The Grove PO10: Westb 6F **23**
PO14: Stub 3D **36**
Grove Apts. *PO8: Cowp* *4F* ***9***
(off Hart Plain Av.)
Grove Av. PO12: Gos 2E **49**
PO16: Portc 5A **28**
Grove Bldgs. PO12: Gos 3E **49**
Grove Ct. PO9: Hav 2F **33**
Grove Ho. PO5: S'sea 6G **5**
(Grove Rd. Sth.)
PO5: S'sea 6H **5** (4D **50**)
(Homegrove Ho.)
Grove Rd. PO6: Dray 4E **31**
PO9: Hav 2F **33**
PO12: Gos 1D **48**
PO13: Lee S 1C **46**
PO16: Fare 2A **26**
Grove Rd. Nth. PO5: S'sea 6G **5** (4D **50**)
Grove Rd. Sth. PO5: S'sea 6G **5** (5C **50**)
Gruneisen Rd. PO2: Ports 3G **41**
Guardhouse Rd. PO1: Ports 6F **41**
Guardians Cl. PO3: Ports 2F **51**
Guardians Way PO3: Ports 2F **51**
Guardroom Rd. PO2: Ports 4F **41**
Guardsman Ct. *PO1: Ports* *2E* ***51***
(off Fratton Rd.)
Gudge Heath La. PO15: Fare 6F **13**
The Guelders PO7: Purb 6G **19**
Guessens La. PO14: Titch 3B **24**
Guildford Cl. PO10: S'brne 2H **35**
Guildford Rd. PO1: Ports 1E **51**
(not continuous)
Guildhall Sq. PO1: Ports 3F **5** (2C **50**)
Guildhall Wlk. PO1: Ports 4E **5** (3C **50**)
Guillemot Gdns. PO13: Gos 2B **38**
Guillemot Pl. PO11: H Isl 6F **55**
Gull Cl. PO13: Gos 3B **38**
Gunners Bldgs. PO3: Ports 1B **42**
Gunners Row PO4: S'sea 5H **51**
Gunners Way PO12: Gos 5F **39**
Gunstore Rd. PO3: Ports 1C **42**
Gunwharf Quays PO1: Ports 4B **4** (3A **50**)
Gunwharf Rd. PO1: Ports 5B **4** (3A **50**)
Gurnard Rd. PO6: Cosh 4A **30**
Gurney Rd. PO4: S'sea 3H **51**
Gutner La. PO11: H Isl 4E **45**
Gutner Point Nature Reserve 5E **45**
Gwatkin Cl. PO9: Bed 6C **20**
Gwynn Way PO17: Wick 1A **14**
Gypsy La. PO8: Cowp 2H **9**

H

Hackett Way *PO14: Fare* *5A* ***26***
(off Sharlands Rd.)
Haddon Cl. PO14: Fare 2G **25**
Hadleigh Rd. PO6: Cosh 3H **29**
Haig Ct. PO2: Ports 2A **42**
Hale Ct. PO1: Ports 6A **42**
Halesowen Ho. PO5: S'sea 5F **5**
Hale St. Nth. PO1: Ports 1D **50**
Hale St. Sth. PO1: Ports 1H **5** (1D **50**)
Half Moon St. PO1: Ports 2B **4** (2A **50**)
Halfpenny La. PO1: Ports 6C **4** (4A **50**)
Halifax Cl. PO14: Titch 1A **24**
Halifax Ri. PO7: W'lle 2H **19**
Hallett Cl. PO9: Warb 1A **34**
Hallett Rd. PO9: Hav 1H **33**
Halletts Cl. PO14: Stub 2E **37**
The Halliards PO16: Fare 4B **26**
Halliday Cl. PO12: Gos 2D **48**
Halliday Cres. PO4: S'sea 4A **52**
Hallowell Ho. PO1: Ports 1C **50**
Halsey Cl. PO12: Gos 4B **48**
Halstead Rd. PO6: Cosh 3H **29**
Halyard Cl. PO13: Gos 6D **38**
Hamble Ct. PO8: Cowp 3H **9**
PO14: Stub 2D **36**
Hambledon Pde. PO7: W'lle 5E **9**
Hambledon Rd. PO7: Den 1A **8**
PO7: W'lle 5E **9**
(not continuous)
PO8: Clan 1E **7**
Hamble Ho. PO16: Fare 4A **26**
Hamble La. PO7: W'lle 4G **19**
Hamble Rd. PO12: Gos 3B **48**
Hambrook Ho. *PO3: Ports* *1G* ***51***
(off Cotton Rd.)
Hambrook Rd. PO12: Gos 1C **48**
Hambrook St. PO5: S'sea 6E **5** (4B **50**)
Hamburg PO1: Ports 1C **4**
Hamfield Dr. PO11: H Isl 3A **54**
Hamilton Cl. PO8: Horn 1B **10**
PO9: Langs 3F **33**
Hamilton Ct. PO5: S'sea 5C **50**
Hamilton Ent. Cen. PO6: Farl 4G **31**
Hamilton Gro. PO13: Gos 3B **38**
Hamilton Ho. *PO1: Ports* *1E* ***51***
(off Clive Rd.)
Hamilton Rd. PO5: S'sea 5D **50**
PO6: Cosh 3C **28**
Ham La. PO8: Cath 5A **6**
PO10: S'brne 4H **35**
PO12: Gos 5G **39**
Hamlet Way PO12: Gos 4G **39**
Hammond Ct. PO12: Gos 3G **49**
Hammond Ind. Est. PO14: Stub 4F **37**
Hammond Rd. PO15: Fare 1F **25**
Hampage Grn. PO9: Hav 2D **20**
Hampshire St. PO1: Ports 6A **42**
Hampshire Ter. PO1: Ports 5E **5** (3B **50**)
Hampton Cl. PO7: W'lle 2A **20**
Hampton Gro. PO15: Fare 2D **24**
Ham Rd. PO17: Boar 3A **16**
Hanbidge Cres. PO13: Gos 1D **38**
Hanbidge Wlk. PO13: Gos 1D **38**
Hanbury Sq. GU31: Pet 2E **57**
Handley Rd. PO12: Gos 1B **48**
Handsworth Ho. PO5: S'sea 4H **5** (3D **50**)
HANGERS EAST 4H **37**
HANGERS WEST 3G **37**

Muccleshell Cl. PO9: Hav 5G 21
Mulberry Av. PO6: Cosh 3C 30
  PO14: Stub 4E 37
Mulberry Cl. PO12: Gos 3D 48
Mulberry Ho. PO5: S'sea 5F 5
Mulberry La. PO6: Cosh 4C 30
Mulberry Lodge PO10: Ems 1D 34
Mulberry Path PO6: Cosh 4C 30
Mullion Cl. PO6: P Sol 4F 29
Mulvany Ct. *PO5: S'sea* 2D 50
  (off Cumberland Rd.)
Mumby Rd. PO12: Gos 2F 49
Mundays Row PO8: Horn 4C 6
Munster Rd. PO2: Ports 3H 41
Murefield Rd. PO1: Ports 2D 50
Muriel Rd. PO7: W'lle 1G 19
Murray Cl. PO15: Fare 1G 25
Murray Rd. PO8: Horn 1B 10
Murray's La. PO1: Ports 1A 4 (1H 49)
Murrills Est. PO16: Portc 3C 28
Muscliffe Cl. PO9: Hav 4H 21
Museum Rd. PO1: Ports 5D 4 (3B 50)
My Lord's La. PO11: H Isl 4D 54
Mynarski VC Rd. PO17: S'wick 3E 17
Myrtle Av. PO16: Portc 4B 28
Myrtle Cl. PO13: Gos 2C 38
Myrtle Gro. PO3: Ports 6D 42

N

Nailsworth Rd. PO6: Cosh 2F 29
Naish Ct. PO9: Hav 2C 20
Naish Dr. PO12: Gos 4G 39
Nancy Rd. PO1: Ports 2E 51
Napier Cl. PO13: Gos 2H 47
Napier Cres. PO15: Fare 2E 25
Napier Rd. PO5: S'sea 5D 50
  PO8: Horn 1C 10
Narborough Ho. PO12: Gos 6B 40
Narvik Rd. PO2: Ports 1H 41
Naseby Cl. PO6: Cosh 2E 29
Nashe Cl. PO15: Fare 6F 13
Nashe Ho. PO15: Fare 6E 13
Nashe Way PO15: Fare 6E 13
Nasmith Cl. PO12: Gos 3A 48
Nat Gonella Sq. *PO12: Gos* 3F 49
  (off Walpole Rd.)
National Mus. Of the Royal Navy Portsmouth
  ....2A 4 (2H 49)
Navy Rd. PO1: Ports 1A 50
Nectar Way PO10: Ems 5E 23
Needles Ho. PO16: Fare 4A 26
Neelands Gro. PO6: Cosh 3C 28
Nelson Av. PO2: Ports 3H 41
  PO16: Portc 4H 27
The Nelson Cen. PO3: Ports 3D 42
Nelson Cl. PO10: S'brne 3E 35
Nelson Ct. PO14: Fare 5H 25
Nelson Cres. PO8: Horn 6C 6
Nelson Dr. GU31: Pet 2E 57
  PO4: S'sea 2A 52
  (not continuous)
Nelson Ho. *PO12: Gos* 3G 49
  (off South St.)
Nelson La. PO17: Fare 6A 16
Nelson Monument 6H 15
Nelson Rd. PO1: Ports 6H 41
  PO5: S'sea 4C 50
  PO9: Bed 2B 32
  PO12: Gos 3D 48
Nepean Cl. PO6: Cosh 6D 48
Neptune Ct. PO1: Ports 5B 4 (3A 50)
  PO13: Gos 3D 38
Neptune Ho. PO6: Cosh 3B 30
Neptune Rd. PO14: Fare 6H 25
  PO15: Fare 1E 25
Nerissa Cl. PO7: W'lle 1A 20
Nesbitt Cl. PO13: Gos 2B 38
Nessus St. PO2: Ports 5H 41
Nest Bus. Pk. PO9: Hav 5H 21
Netherfield Cl. PO9: Warb 2G 33
Netherton Rd. PO12: Gos 6F 39
Netley Ct. PO12: Gos 5A 40
Netley Pl. *PO5: S'sea* 5C 50
  (off Netley Ter.)
Netley Rd. PO5: S'sea 5C 50
Netley Ter. PO5: S'sea 5C 50
Nettlecombe Av. PO4: S'sea 6E 51
Nettlestone Rd. PO4: S'sea 5G 51
Neville Av. PO16: Portc 5B 28
Neville Ct. PO12: Gos 2D 48

Neville Gdns. PO10: Ems 6C 22
Neville Rd. PO3: Ports 6C 42
Nevil Shute Rd. PO3: Ports 2C 42
Nevinson Way PO7: Purb 4E 19
New Barn Farm La. PO8: Blen 3E 7, 2D 6
Newbarn Rd. PO9: Bed 6B 20
Newbolt Cl. PO8: Cowp 4G 9
Newbolt Rd. PO6: Cosh 2C 28
NEW BRIGHTON 6D 22
New Brighton Rd. PO10: Ems 2D 34
Newbroke Rd. PO13: Gos 5D 38
Newcomen Ct. PO2: Ports 3G 41
Newcomen Rd. PO2: Ports 3G 41
Newcome Rd. PO1: Ports 1E 51
New Cut PO11: H Isl 2B 44
New Down La. PO7: Purb 1C 30
Newgate La. PO14: Fare 2A 38
Newgate La. Ind. Est. PO14: Fare 5B 26
  (not continuous)
New Hampshire Blvd. 4B 4 (3A 50)
Newlands PO15: Fare 2E 25
Newlands Av. PO7: Purb 4E 19
  PO12: Gos 3C 48
Newlands La. PO7: Den, Purb 5B 8
Newlands Rd. PO7: Purb 4F 19
New La. PO9: Hav 1G 33
Newlease Rd. PO7: W'lle 4H 19
Newlyn Way PO6: P Sol 4E 29
Newmer Ct. PO9: Hav 3C 20
Newney Cl. PO2: Ports 1B 42
Newnham Ct. PO9: Hav 4H 21
New Pde. PO16: Portc 3B 28
Newport Rd. PO12: Gos 2B 48
New Priory Gdns. PO16: Portc 3A 28
New Rd. PO2: Ports 6A 42
  PO8: Clan 1C 6
  PO8: Love 1G 9
  PO9: Bed, Hav 1D 32
  PO10: S'brne 3H 35
  PO10: Westb 6F 23
  PO16: Fare 2A 26
New Rd. E. PO2: Ports 5B 42
New Royal Theatre 3E 5 (2C 50)
The News Cen. PO3: Ports 6B 30
Newton Cl. PO14: Stub 1E 37
Newton Pl. PO13: Lee S 6G 37
NEWTOWN
  PO11 ....3A 54
  PO12 ....3E 49
Newtown PO16: Portc 3B 28
Newtown La. PO11: H Isl 3A 54
Nicholas Ct. PO11: H Isl 4A 54
  PO13: Lee S 2C 46
Nicholas Cres. PO15: Fare 1H 25
Nicholson Gdns. PO1: Ports 2H 5
Nicholson Way PO9: Hav 6E 21
Nickel St. PO5: S'sea 6E 5 (4B 50)
Nickleby Ho. PO1: Ports 6H 41
Nickleby Rd. PO8: Clan 1F 7
Nightingale Cl. PO9: R Cas 6G 11
  PO12: Gos 1B 48
Nightingale Ct. PO6: Cosh 3D 30
  PO10: Westb 5F 23
Nightingale Lodge PO8: Cowp 4A 10
Nightingale Pk. PO9: Warb 2H 33
Nightingale Rd. GU32: Pet 5C 56
  PO5: S'sea 5B 50
  PO6: Cosh 2B 30
Nightjar Cl. PO8: Horn 6A 6
Nile Ho. PO16: Fare 2F 27
Nile St. PO10: Ems 3D 34
Nimrod Dr. PO13: Gos 1H 47
Nine Elms La. PO17: Fare 5D 14
Ninian Pk. Rd. PO3: Ports 3C 42
Ninian Path PO3: Ports 3C 42
Niton Cl. PO13: Gos 3C 38
Nobbs La. PO1: Ports 5C 4 (3A 50)
Nobes Av. PO13: Gos 2C 38
Nobes Cl. PO13: Gos 3D 38
Noctule Ct. PO17: K Vil 1F 13
The Nook PO13: Gos 4E 39
Norden Way PO9: Hav 4C 20
Nore Cres. PO10: Ems 2B 34
Nore Farm Av. PO10: Ems 2B 34
Noreuil Rd. GU32: Pet 4B 56
Norfolk Ho. PO9: Hav 2G 33
Norfolk M. PO11: H Isl 4A 54
Norfolk Rd. PO12: Gos 6F 39
Norfolk St. PO5: S'sea 6F 5 (4C 50)
Norgett Way PO16: Portc 5H 27
Norland Rd. PO4: S'sea 4E 51
Norley Cl. PO9: Hav 4E 21

Norman Cl. PO16: Portc 5B 28
Norman Ct. PO4: S'sea 5E 51
Normandy Ct. PO17: Wick 1B 14
Normandy Gdns. PO12: Gos 3B 48
Normandy Rd. PO2: Ports 1H 41
  PO14: Fare 3G 25
Norman Rd. PO4: S'sea 4E 51
  PO11: H Isl 5D 54
  PO12: Gos 2C 48
Norman Way PO9: Bed 1C 32
Norris Gdns. PO9: Warb 3G 33
Norrish Ct. *PO1: Ports* 6A 42
  (off Inverness Rd.)
Norset Rd. PO15: Fare 1E 25
Northam M. PO1: Ports 2H 5 (2D 50)
Northam St. PO1: Ports 1H 5 (1D 50)
Northarbour Rd. PO6: Cosh 4H 29
Northarbour Spur PO6: Cosh 3H 29
Nth Av. PO2: Ports 6A 30
Nth. Battery Rd. PO2: Ports 3F 41
Northbrook Cl. PO1: Ports 6H 41
North Bldg. PO1: Ports 3A 4
North Cl. PO9: Hav 3G 33
  PO12: Gos 3B 48
Northcote Gdns. PO10: S'brne 3H 35
Northcote Rd. PO4: S'sea 4E 51
Northcott Cl. PO12: Gos 4B 48
North Ct. PO1: Ports 6A 42
North Cres. PO11: H Isl 4D 54
Northcroft Rd. PO12: Gos 1B 48
Nth. Cross St. PO12: Gos 3F 49
North Dr. PO17: S'wick 3D 16
NORTH END 4H 41
Nth. End Av. PO2: Ports 3H 41
Northern Pde. PO2: Ports 2H 41
Northern Rd. PO6: Cosh 5B 30
Northesk Ho. PO1: Ports 1D 50
NORTH FAREHAM 5B 14
Northfield Av. PO14: Fare 4H 25
Northfield Cvn. Pk. 1H 27
Northfield Cl. PO8: Horn 3C 6
Northfield Pk. PO16: Portc 2H 27
Northgate Av. PO2: Ports 5B 42
North Gro. Ho. PO5: S'sea 6H 5 (4D 50)
NORTH HARBOUR 5F 29
Nth. Harbour Bus. Pk. PO6: Cosh 4G 29
NORTH HAYLING 2E 45
North Hill PO16: Fare 6B 14
  PO17: S'wick 1F 29
Northlands Pk. PO10: Ems 2E 35
North La. PO8: Clan 1F 7
Nth. Meadow *PO12: Gos* 1F 49
  (off Weevil La.)
NORTHNEY 1E 45
Northney La. PO11: H Isl 1E 45
Northney Marina 6H 33
Northney Rd. PO11: H Isl 6G 33
Northover Ho. PO3: Ports 5D 42
North Pk. Bus. Cen. PO17: K Vil 1F 13
Nth. Promenade Bldg. PO1: Ports 4A 4
North Rd. GU32: Pet 3D 56
  PO8: Horn 3C 6
  PO17: S'wick 1E 29
North Rd. E. PO17: S'wick 3E 17
North Rd. W. PO17: S'wick 3D 16
Nth. Shore Rd. PO11: H Isl 3H 53
North Sq. PO17: K Vil 2G 13
North St. PO1: Ports 1D 50
  (Cornwallis Cres.)
  PO1: Ports 2C 4 (2A 50)
  (Sarah Robinson Ho.)
  PO9: Bed 1D 32
  PO9: Hav 2F 33
  PO10: Ems 2D 34
  PO10: Westb 4F 23
  PO12: Gos 3F 49
  (not continuous)
North St. Arc. PO9: Hav 2F 33
Northumberland Rd. PO5: S'sea 3E 51
NORTH WALLINGTON 1D 26
North Wallington PO16: Fare 1C 26
North Way PO9: Hav 2E 33
Northway PO13: Gos 1C 38
  PO15: Titch 6A 12
Northways PO14: Stub 3F 37
Northwood La. PO11: H Isl 4C 44
Northwood Rd. PO2: Ports 1A 42
Northwood Sq. PO16: Fare 1B 26
Norton Cl. PO7: W'lle 2F 19
  PO17: S'wick 3D 16
Norton Dr. PO16: Fare 6A 14
Norton Rd. PO17: S'wick 3D 16

Norway Rd.—Pan St.

Norway Rd. PO3: Ports 1B **42**
Norwich Pl. PO13: Lee S 6G **37**
Norwich Rd. PO6: Cosh 2H **29**
Nottingham Pl. PO13: Lee S 6G **37**
Novello Gdns. PO7: W'lle 3G **19**
Nuffield Health
Portsmouth *2H 41*
(off Alex Way)
Nursery Cl. PO10: Ems 6D **22**
PO13: Gos 2B **38**
Nursery Gdns. PO8: Horn 2A **10**
Nursery La. PO14: Stub 3E **37**
Nursery Rd. PO9: Bed 1C **32**
Nursling Cres. PO9: Hav 4G **21**
Nutbourne Ho. PO6: Farl 4F **31**
Nutbourne Rd. PO6: Farl 4F **31**
PO11: H Isl 5G **55**
Nutfield Ct. PO1: Ports 1E **51**
Nutfield Pl. PO1: Ports 1D **50**
Nuthatch Cl. PO9: R Cas 6H **11**
Nutley Rd. PO9: Hav 4D **20**
Nutwick Rd. PO9: Hav 6H **21**
Nyewood Av. PO16: Portc 2B **28**
Nyria Way PO12: Gos 3F **49**

O

Oakapple Gdns. PO6: Farl 3G **31**
Oak Cl. PO8: Cowp 5G **9**
Oak Ct. PO15: Fare 1E **25**
Oakcroft La. PO14: Stub 6E **25**
Oakdene PO13: Gos 4D **38**
Oakdene Rd. PO4: S'sea 3A **52**
Oakdown Rd. PO14: Stub 2F **37**
Oak Dr. GU31: Pet 6C **56**
The Oakes PO14: Stub 1D **36**
Oakfield Ct. PO9: Hav 4H **21**
Oakhurst Dr. PO7: W'lle 1A **20**
Oakhurst Gdns. PO7: Wid 1D **30**
Oaklands PO7: W'lle 3A **20**
Oaklands Av. PO9: R Cas 6H **11**
Oaklands Gro. PO8: Cowp 4F **9**
Oaklands Ho. PO6: Cosh 1D **28**
Oaklands Rd. GU32: Pet 3C **56**
PO9: Hav 2G **33**
Oaklea Cl. PO7: Wid 1D **30**
Oakleaf Way PO8: Horn 1D **10**
Oakley Gdns. PO7: Wid 6E **19**
Oakley Ho. PO5: S'sea 6F **5**
Oakley Rd. PO9: Hav 4D **20**
Oak Lodge PO2: Ports 3G **41**
Oakmeadow Cl. PO10: Ems 6E **23**
Oakmont Dr. PO8: Cowp 5H **9**
OAK PARK *6F 21*
Oak Pk. Dr. PO9: Hav 6G **21**
Oak Pk. Ind. Est. PO6: Cosh 3H **29**
Oak Rd. PO8: Clan 2G **7**
PO15: Fare 1F **25**
The Oaks PO8: Cowp 5A **10**
Oaks Coppice PO8: Horn 1A **10**
The Oaks Havant Crematorium 4A **22**
Oakshott Dr. PO9: Hav 4G **21**
Oak St. PO12: Gos 3E **49**
Oakthorn Cl. PO13: Gos 1G **47**
Oak Tree Dr. PO10: Ems 5C **22**
Oakum Ho. PO3: Ports 1G **51**
Oakwood Av. PO9: Bed 6B **20**
The Oakwood Cen. PO9: Hav 5H **21**
Oakwood Rd. PO2: Ports 1A **42**
PO11: H Isl 4B **54**
Oasthouse Dr. PO8: Horn 6D **6**
Oberon Cl. PO7: W'lle 1A **20**
Occupation La. PO14: Titch 3A **24**
Ocean Cl. PO15: Fare 1F **25**
Ocean Ct. PO11: H Isl 5A **54**
Ocean Pk. PO3: Ports 3D **42**
Ocean Rd. PO14: Fare 6H **25**
Ockendon Cl. PO5: S'sea 5F **5** (3C **50**)
Octavius Ct. PO7: W'lle 6B **10**
Odell Cl. PO16: Fare 6H **13**
Odeon Cinema
Port Solent 5F **29**
The Officers Quarters PO12: Gos 2F **49**
O'Jays Ind. Pk. PO3: Ports 3C **42**
Olave Cl. PO13: Lee S 1C **46**
The Old Bakery *PO4: S'sea* *5E 51*
(off Waverley Rd.)
Old Barn Gdns. PO8: Love 1H **9**
The Old Brewery PO8: Horn 6D **6**
Old Brewery Way PO8: Horn 6D **6**
Old Bri. Rd. PO4: S'sea 5E **51**
Oldbury Ho. PO5: S'sea 5F **5**
Oldbury Way PO14: Fare 3E **25**
Old Canal PO4: S'sea 3H **51**
(not continuous)
Old College Wlk. PO6: Cosh 5C **30**
Old Commercial Rd. PO1: Ports 6G **41**
Old Copse Rd. PO9: Hav 1G **33**
Oldcroft Ct. PO9: Hav 2E **33**
Old Dairy Workshops
PO10: Westb 6F **23**
Old Drum M. GU32: Pet 4D **56**
Old Farm La. PO10: Westb 6F **23**
PO14: Stub 4E **37**
Old Farm Way PO6: Farl 4G **31**
The Old Flour Mill PO10: Ems 3E **35**
Oldgate Gdns. PO2: Ports 1B **42**
Old Gosport Rd. PO16: Fare 3B **26**
Old Infirmary Ho. PO1: Ports 5B **4**
Old La. PO8: Cath 3B **6**
Old London Rd. PO2: Ports 1B **42**
Old Manor Farm PO9: Bed 2B **32**
Old Mnr. Way PO6: Cosh 4D **30**
Old Mill La. GU31: Pet 2F **57**
PO8: Love 1D **8**
Old Orchard PO7: W'lle 1H **19**
OLD PORTSMOUTH 6B **4** (4A **50**)
The Old Railway PO12: Gos 2E **49**
Old Rectory Cl. PO10: Westb 6E **23**
Old Rectory Rd. PO6: Farl 3G **31**
Old Reservoir Rd. PO6: Farl 4F **31**
Old River PO7: Den 4B **8**
Old Rd. PO12: Gos 4E **49**
The Old Road PO6: Cosh 5B **30**
Old School Ct. PO16: Fare 1C **26**
Old School Dr. PO11: H Isl 5D **54**
Old Spot Cnr. PO7: W'lle 6E **9**
Old Star Pl. PO1: Ports 2B **4** (2A **50**)
Old St. PO14: Stub 4C **36**
(not continuous)
Old Timbers PO11: H Isl 4B **54**
Old Turnpike PO16: Fare 6B **14**
Old Van Diemans Rd. PO7: Purb 4E **19**
Old Wymering La. PO6: Cosh 3A **30**
Olinda St. PO1: Ports 1E **51**
Olive Cres. PO16: Portc 5B **28**
Olive Leaf Ct. PO11: H Isl 2D **54**
Oliver Ct. PO12: Gos 3E **49**
Oliver Rd. PO4: S'sea 4G **51**
Olivers Ct. PO2: Ports 5A **42**
Olivia Cl. PO7: W'lle 6A **10**
Omega Ho. PO5: S'sea 3H **5** (2D **50**)
Omega St. PO5: S'sea 3H **5** (2D **50**)
Onslow Rd. PO5: S'sea 6D **50**
Ophir Rd. PO2: Ports 3H **41**
Oracle Dr. PO7: Purb 6G **19**
Orange Gro. PO13: Gos 4D **38**
Orange Row PO10: Ems 3D **34**
The Orchard PO6: Cosh 4B **30**
PO7: Den 3B **8**
Orchard Cl. PO8: Horn 1C **10**
PO11: H Isl 5B **54**
PO12: Gos 4G **39**
Orchard Ga. PO6: Dray 3D **30**
Orchard Gro. PO8: Cowp 4H **9**
PO16: Portc 4G **27**
Orchard La. PO10: S'brne 3E **35**
Orchard Mead PO7: W'lle 1E **19**
Orchard Rd. PO4: S'sea 3E **51**
PO9: Hav 3F **33**
PO11: H Isl 5C **54**
Orchard Way GU31: Pet 6D **56**
Orchid Cl. PO17: K Vil 2F **13**
Orchid Dr. PO10: Ems 5E **23**
Ordnance Bus. Pk.
PO13: Gos 2D **38**
Ordnance Ct. PO3: Ports 6C **30**
Ordnance Rd. PO12: Gos 3F **49**
Ordnance Row PO1: Ports 3B **4** (2A **50**)
Orford Ct. PO6: Cosh 4B **30**
Oriel Rd. PO2: Ports 3H **41**
Orion Av. PO12: Gos 6A **40**
Orion Cl. PO14: Stub 3F **37**
Orkney Rd. PO6: Cosh 2B **30**
Orme Ct. PO16: Fare 2A **26**
Ormsby Rd. PO5: S'sea 4C **50**
Ornamental Farm 3G **21**
Orpine Cl. PO15: Titch 6B **12**
Orsmond Cl. PO7: W'lle 3H **19**
Orsted Dr. PO6: Dray 5D **30**
Orwell Cl. PO12: Gos 6A **40**
Orwell Rd. GU31: Pet 5C **56**
Osborn Ct. PO3: Ports 1D **42**
Osborn Cres. PO13: Gos 1B **38**
Osborne Cl. PO7: W'lle 2A **20**
Osborne Rd. GU32: Pet 3D **56**
PO5: S'sea 5C **50**
PO12: Gos 2F **49**
PO13: Lee S 1C **46**
Osborne Vw. Rd. PO14: Stub 4C **36**
Osborn Mall PO16: Fare 2C **26**
Osborn Rd. PO16: Fare 2B **26**
Osborn Rd. Sth. PO16: Fare 2B **26**
Osborn Sq. PO16: Fare 2C **26**
Osier Cl. PO2: Ports 3G **41**
Osier Rd. GU32: Pet 5B **56**
Osmond Ho. PO9: Hav 2D **32**
Osprey Cl. PO6: Farl 4H **31**
Osprey Ct. PO4: S'sea 2H **51**
PO16: Portc 3F **27**
Osprey Dr. PO11: H Isl 4D **54**
Osprey Gdns. PO13: Lee S 1D **46**
Osprey Quay PO10: S'brne 4F **35**
Othello Dr. PO7: W'lle 1A **20**
Otterbourne Cres. PO9: Hav 4D **20**
Otter Cl. PO13: Gos 2H **47**
Otter Wlk. 6B **56**
Outlook PO4: S'sea 3F **51**
Outram Rd. PO5: S'sea 6H **5** (4D **50**)
Oval Gdns. PO12: Gos 3B **48**
The Oven Camp Site 2B **54**
Overton Cres. PO9: Hav 4D **20**
Overton Rd. PO10: S'brne 2H **35**
Owen Cl. PO13: Gos 6C **38**
PO16: Fare 6B **14**
Owen Ho. *PO3: Ports* *1F 51*
(off Whitcombe Gdns.)
Owen St. PO4: S'sea 5G **51**
Owslebury Gro. PO9: Hav 4F **21**
Oxenwood Grn. PO9: Hav 3D **20**
Oxford Cl. PO16: Fare 1H **25**
Oxford Rd. PO5: S'sea 4E **51**
PO12: Gos 2B **48**
Oxleys Cl. PO14: Fare 3D **24**
Oxted Ct. PO4: S'sea 2H **51**
Oysell Gdns. PO16: Fare 2F **27**
Oyster Cl. PO11: H Isl 4D **54**
Oyster Est. PO6: Farl 4F **31**
Oyster M. PO1: Ports 6B **4** (4A **50**)
Oyster Quay PO6: P Sol 4F **29**
Oyster St. PO1: Ports 6B **4** (4A **50**)
Oyster Vw. PO13: Lee S 6F **37**

P

Padbury Cl. PO2: Ports 1B **42**
Paddington Rd. PO2: Ports 4B **42**
The Paddock PO12: Gos 4C **48**
PO14: Stub 1E **37**
Paddock End PO7: Den 4B **8**
Paddock Wlk. PO6: Cosh 3E **29**
Paddock Way GU32: Pet 5B **56**
Padnell Av. PO8: Cowp 4A **10**
Padnell Pl. PO8: Cowp 5B **10**
Padnell Rd. PO8: Cowp 4A **10**
Padwick Av. PO6: Cosh 3C **30**
Padwick Ct. PO11: H Isl 4A **54**
Paffard Cl. PO13: Gos 6C **38**
Paget Rd. PO12: Gos 5C **48**
Pagham Cl. PO10: S'brne 3E **35**
Pagham Gdns. PO11: H Isl 5H **55**
Paignton Av. PO3: Ports 5C **42**
Pain's Rd. PO5: S'sea 5H **5** (3D **50**)
Painswick Cl. PO6: Cosh 3G **29**
Painter Cl. PO3: Ports 2D **42**
Palk Rd. PO9: Bed 1D **32**
The Pallant PO9: Hav 2F **33**
Pallant Gdns. PO16: Fare 1D **26**
Palm Ct. PO5: S'sea 5C **50**
Palmer's Rd. PO10: Ems 2D **34**
Palmers Rd. Ind. Est. PO10: Ems 2D **34**
Palmerston Av. PO16: Fare 2B **26**
Palmerston Bus. Pk. PO14: Fare 4A **26**
Palmerston Ct. *PO5: S'sea* *5C 50*
(off Clarence Pde.)
Palmerston Dr. PO14: Fare 4A **26**
Palmerston Indoor Bowls Club 4A **26**
Palmerston Mans. *PO5: S'sea* *5C 50*
(off Palmerston Rd.)
Palmerston Rd. PO5: S'sea 5C **50**
PO11: H Isl 3C **54**
Palmerston Way PO12: Gos 5A **48**
Palmyra Rd. PO12: Gos 6G **39**
Pamela Av. PO6: Cosh 2D **28**
Pangbourne Av. PO6: Cosh 4D **30**
Pannall Rd. PO12: Gos 6G **39**
Pan St. PO1: Ports 1G **5** (1C **50**)

A-Z Portsmouth 79

Panton Cl.—Poplar Gro.

Panton Cl. PO10: Ems . . . 6C **22**
The Parade PO1: Ports . . . 1B **4** (1A **50**)
PO13: Gos . . . 2B **38**
PO14: Stub . . . 2E **37**
Parade Ct. PO2: Ports . . . 6A **30**
Paradise La. PO10: Westb . . . 5F **23**
PO16: Fare . . . 2E **27**
(not continuous)
Paradise St. PO1: Ports . . . 1G **5** (1C **50**)
The Parchment PO9: Hav . . . 2F **33**
Parham Pl. PO10: S'brne . . . 3G **35**
Parham Rd. PO12: Gos . . . 1E **49**
Park & Ride
Tipner . . . **2G 41**
Park App. PO17: K Vil . . . 2G **13**
Park Av. PO7: Purb, Wid . . . 1E **31**
Park Cl. PO12: Gos . . . 1B **48**
Park Cottage Dr. PO15: Seg . . . 6B **12**
Park Ct. PO5: S'sea . . . 6F **5** (4C **50**)
Park Cres. PO10: Ems . . . 2B **34**
Parker Cl. PO12: Gos . . . 4G **39**
Parker Gdns. PO7: Wid . . . 1E **31**
Parkers Trade Pk. GU32: Pet . . . 4B **56**
Parker View PO16: Fare . . . 4A **26**
Park Farm Av. PO15: Fare . . . 5E **13**
Park Farm Cl. PO15: Fare . . . 6F **13**
Park Farm Rd. PO7: Purb . . . 5F **19**
Parkfield Ho. PO6: Cosh . . . 1D **28**
Park Gro. PO6: Cosh . . . 4B **30**
Park Ho. PO5: S'sea . . . 5C **50**
Park Ho. Farm Way PO9: Hav . . . 5B **20**
Parklands PO7: Den . . . 4B **8**
Parklands Av. PO8: Cowp . . . 2A **10**
PO8: Horn . . . 2A **10**
Parklands Bus. Pk. PO7: Den . . . 4B **8**
Parklands Cl. PO12: Gos . . . 1D **48**
Park La. PO6: Cosh . . . 3C **30**
PO7: W'lle . . . 6B **10**
PO8: Cowp . . . 5A **10**
PO9: Bed . . . 1C **32**
PO9: Hav . . . 1C **20**
PO10: R Cas . . . 1F **23**
PO14: Stub . . . 2E **37**
PO16: Fare . . . 1B **26**
Park Mans. PO6: Cosh . . . 4C **30**
Park Pde. PO9: Hav . . . 5E **21**
Park Rd. GU32: Pet . . . 4D **56**
PO1: Ports . . . 4C **4** (3A **50**)
PO7: Den . . . 2B **8**
PO7: Purb . . . 5E **19**
PO10: S'brne . . . 2H **35**
PO11: H Isl . . . 3G **53**
PO12: Gos . . . 5D **48**
Park Rd. Nth. PO9: Hav . . . 1E **33**
Park Rd. Sth. PO9: Hav . . . 2F **33**
Park Royal PO2: Ports . . . 2A **42**
Parkside PO9: Bed . . . 1C **32**
Parkside Cl. PO7: Purb . . . 5E **19**
Parkstone Av. PO4: S'sea . . . 6E **51**
Parkstone La. PO4: S'sea . . . 5E **51**
Park St. PO5: S'sea . . . 5E **5** (3B **50**)
PO12: Gos . . . 2D **48**
Park Terraces PO12: Gos . . . 3E **49**
Park Vw. PO9: R Cas . . . 1H **21**
Park Vw. Ho. PO16: Fare . . . 5B **14**
Park Wlk. PO15: Fare . . . 6F **13**
Park Way PO9: Hav . . . 2E **33**
Parkway PO15: White . . . 2A **12**
PO16: Fare . . . 6B **14**
The Parkway PO3: Ports . . . 1F **51**
PO13: Gos . . . 3B **38**
Parkwood Cen. PO7: W'lle . . . 1G **19**
Parr Rd. PO6: Cosh . . . 3H **29**
Parry Cl. PO6: Cosh . . . 3C **28**
Parry Ct. PO12: Gos . . . 2E **49**
Parsonage Cl. GU32: Pet . . . 2F **57**
Parsons Cl. PO3: Ports . . . 1B **42**
The Partnership Bus. Pk. PO4: S'sea . . . 2F **51**
Partridge Cl. PO16: Portc . . . 3E **27**
Partridge Gdns. PO8: Cowp . . . 3F **9**
Passfield Wlk. PO9: Hav . . . 4H **21**
Passingham Wlk. PO8: Cowp . . . 3A **10**
Pasteur Rd. PO6: Cosh . . . 3A **30**
The Pastures PO7: Den . . . 3A **8**
Patchway Dr. PO14: Fare . . . 3E **25**
Patrick Howard Dobson Ct. PO8: Cowp . . . 3H **9**
Patterdale Ho. PO6: Cosh . . . 2F **29**
Pattersons La. PO8: Blen . . . 1E **11**
PAULSGROVE . . . **3F 29**
Paulsgrove Ent. Cen. PO6: Cosh . . . 3F **29**
Paulsgrove Ind. Cen. PO6: Cosh . . . 3F **29**
Paulsgrove Rd. PO2: Ports . . . 5B **42**
Pavant M. PO9: Hav . . . 2F **33**
Pavilion Way PO12: Gos . . . 2F **49**
Paxton Rd. PO14: Fare . . . 2H **25**
Peacock Cl. PO16: Portc . . . 3E **27**
Peacock Gdns. PO8: Horn . . . 2B **10**
Peacock La. PO1: Ports . . . 6C **4** (4A **50**)
The Peak PO9: R Cas . . . 4H **11**
Peak Dr. PO14: Fare . . . 3F **25**
Peakfield PO7: Den . . . 3A **8**
Peak La. PO14: Fare . . . 3F **25**
Peak Rd. PO8: Clan . . . 2E **7**
Pearce Ct. PO12: Gos . . . 2E **49**
Pearmain Pde. PO7: W'lle . . . 2E **19**
Pears Gro. PO10: S'brne . . . 3H **35**
Pearson Ho. PO12: Gos . . . 6B **40**
Peartree Cl. PO14: Stub . . . 2F **37**
Peasgood La. PO7: W'lle . . . 2F **19**
Pebble Beach Apts. PO13: Lee S . . . 2C **46**
Pebble Cl. PO11: H Isl . . . 5D **54**
Pebble Ct. PO11: H Isl . . . 6F **55**
Pebmarsh Rd. PO6: Cosh . . . 3H **29**
Pedam Cl. PO4: S'sea . . . 4G **51**
PEEL COMMON . . . **3A 38**
Peelers Ga. PO6: Cosh . . . 4B **30**
Peel Pl. PO5: S'sea . . . 5F **5** (3C **50**)
Peel Rd. PO12: Gos . . . 2E **49**
Pegasus Cl. PO13: Gos . . . 2H **47**
Peggotty Ho. PO1: Ports . . . 6H **41**
Pegham Ind. Pk. PO15: F'ley . . . 3E **13**
Pelham Rd. PO5: S'sea . . . 6G **5** (4C **50**)
PO12: Gos . . . 2D **48**
Pelham Rd. Pas. PO5: S'sea . . . 6G **5** (4C **50**)
Pelham Ter. PO10: Ems . . . 3E **35**
Pelican Cl. PO15: Fare . . . 1F **25**
Pelican Rd. PO14: Fare . . . 6H **25**
Pembroke Chambers PO1: Ports . . . 6C **4**
Pembroke Cl. PO1: Ports . . . 6C **4** (4A **50**)
Pembroke Ct. PO13: Gos . . . 4C **38**
Pembroke Cres. PO14: Stub . . . 3C **36**
Pembroke Rd. PO1: Ports . . . 6C **4** (4A **50**)
(not continuous)
Pembury Rd. PO9: Warb . . . 3G **33**
PO14: Stub . . . 1F **37**
Penarth Av. PO6: Dray . . . 3D **30**
Pendennis Rd. PO6: Cosh . . . 2D **28**
Pendragon Apts. PO5: S'sea . . . 6D **50**
Penfold Way PO9: Hav . . . 3C **20**
Penhale Rd. PO1: Ports . . . 2E **51**
Penhurst Rd. PO9: Bed . . . 1B **32**
Penjar Av. PO7: Purb . . . 5E **19**
Penk Ridge PO9: Bed . . . 3H **31**
Pennant Hills PO9: Bed . . . 1B **32**
Pennant Pk. PO16: Fare . . . 6C **14**
Pennerly Ct. PO9: Hav . . . 2D **20**
Penner Rd. PO9: Hav . . . 4E **33**
Pennine Wlk. PO14: Fare . . . 4G **25**
Pennine Way PO13: Lee S . . . 3E **47**
Pennington Way PO15: Fare . . . 6F **13**
Penns Pl. GU31: Pet . . . 3H **57**
Penns Rd. GU32: Pet . . . 3C **56**
Penn Way PO12: Gos . . . 4A **48**
Penny Ct. *PO12: Gos . . . 2E 49*
(off Ferrol Rd.)
Penny La. PO10: S'brne . . . 3F **35**
Penny Pl. PO7: Purb . . . 6G **19**
Penny St. PO1: Ports . . . 6B **4** (4A **50**)
Penrhyn Av. PO6: Dray . . . 3D **30**
Penrose Cl. PO2: Ports . . . 3H **41**
Pentere Rd. PO8: Horn . . . 1A **10**
Pentland Ri. PO16: Portc . . . 2B **28**
Penton Ct. PO9: Hav . . . 3H **21**
Penwood Grn. PO9: Hav . . . 4H **21**
Peper Harow PO8: Horn . . . 1B **10**
Pepper Cl. PO11: H Isl . . . 2C **54**
Pepys Cl. PO4: S'sea . . . 4F **51**
PO12: Gos . . . 6D **48**
Percival Cl. PO13: Lee S . . . 2E **47**
Percival Rd. PO2: Ports . . . 5B **42**
Percy Chandler St. PO1: Ports . . . 1H **5** (1D **50**)
Percy Rd. PO4: S'sea . . . 3E **51**
PO12: Gos . . . 3E **49**
The Peregrines PO16: Portc . . . 3F **27**
Perkins Ho. PO1: Ports . . . 2D **4**
Peronne Cl. PO3: Ports . . . 6B **30**
Peronne Rd. PO3: Ports . . . 6B **30**
Perseus Pl. PO7: Purb . . . 6G **19**
Perseus Ter. PO1: Ports . . . 5B **4** (3A **50**)
Perth Ho. PO1: Ports . . . 2H **5** (2D **50**)
Perth Rd. PO4: S'sea . . . 3H **51**
PO13: Gos . . . 2D **38**
Pervin Rd. PO6: Cosh . . . 3B **30**
Peter Ashley Activity Cen. . . . **2F 31**
Peter Ashley La. PO6: Dray . . . 2F **31**
Peterborough Rd. PO6: Cosh . . . 2A **30**
PETERSFIELD . . . **4D 56**
Petersfield Bus. Pk. GU32: Pet . . . 4B **56**
PETERSFIELD COMMUNITY HOSPITAL . . . **4C 56**
Petersfield Ho. PO1: Ports . . . 1H **5**
Petersfield La. PO8: Clan . . . 1G **7**
Petersfield Mus. . . . **4D 56**
Petersfield (Old) Golf Course . . . **6E 57**
Petersfield Open Air Swimming Pool . . . **4E 57**
Petersfield Physic Garden . . . **4D 56**
Petersfield Rd. PO9: Hav . . . 1E **33**
Petersfield Station (Rail) . . . **3C 56**
Petersham Cl. PO7: W'lle . . . 6F **9**
Petersham Ho. *PO5: S'sea . . . 6D 50*
(off Clarendon Rd.)
Petrel Wlk. PO13: Gos . . . 3B **38**
Petrie Rd. PO13: Lee S . . . 1D **46**
Pettycot Cres. PO13: Gos . . . 2B **38**
Petworth Rd. PO3: Ports . . . 1H **51**
Philip Rd. PO7: W'lle . . . 4H **19**
Phoenix Bldgs. PO3: Ports . . . 3C **42**
Phoenix Ct. PO5: S'sea . . . 6H **5** (4D **50**)
Phoenix Sq. PO2: Ports . . . 1A **42**
Phoenix Way PO13: Gos . . . 4C **38**
Pickwick Ho. PO1: Ports . . . 6H **41**
Picton Ho. PO5: S'sea . . . 4G **5** (3C **50**)
PO7: W'lle . . . 6E **9**
Pier Head Rd. PO2: Ports . . . 5E **41**
Pier Ho. PO13: Lee S . . . 1C **46**
Pier Rd. PO5: S'sea . . . 5B **50**
Pier St. PO13: Lee S . . . 1C **46**
Pigeon Ho. La. PO7: Purb . . . 3H **17**
Piggott Pl. GU31: Pet . . . 2F **57**
Pilbrow Ct. PO12: Gos . . . 3B **48**
Pilgrims Way PO14: Stub . . . 4D **36**
Pilning Cl. PO14: Fare . . . 3E **25**
Pimpernel Way *PO7: W'lle . . . 6E 9*
(off Melick Way)
Pine Ct. PO10: Ems . . . 5D **22**
Pine Dr. PO8: Clan . . . 2G **7**
Pine Gro. PO9: Hav . . . 2G **33**
Pinehurst Cl. PO7: W'lle . . . 5C **10**
The Pines PO16: Fare . . . 2G **27**
Pine Tree Gdns. PO8: Cowp . . . 5A **10**
Pine Trees Cl. PO14: Fare . . . 3F **25**
Pine Tree Wlk. PO8: Horn . . . 2D **6**
Pinewood PO13: Gos . . . 4E **39**
Pinewood Av. PO9: Bed . . . 6B **20**
Pinewood Cl. PO14: Stub . . . 1F **37**
Pinewood Lodge *PO16: Fare . . . 1B 26*
(off Southampton Rd.)
Pink Ct. PO1: Ports . . . 2E **51**
Pink Rd. PO2: Ports . . . 5A **42**
Pinks Hill PO16: Fare . . . 1D **26**
Pinsley Dr. PO17: S'wick . . . 3D **16**
Pipers Mead PO8: Clan . . . 2E **7**
Pipers Wood Ind. Pk. PO7: W'lle . . . 1E **19**
Pipistrelle Wlk. PO17: K Vil . . . 1G **13**
Pipit Cl. PO8: Horn . . . 1A **10**
PO12: Gos . . . 6H **39**
Pipits Cl. PO9: Hav . . . 5D **20**
Pitcairn M. PO4: S'sea . . . 5H **51**
Pitcroft La. PO2: Ports . . . 5H **41**
(not continuous)
Pitcroft Rd. PO2: Ports . . . 4H **41**
Pitreavie Rd. PO6: Cosh . . . 5B **30**
Pitymoor La. PO17: S'wick . . . 5F **17**
Place Cres. PO7: W'lle . . . 4H **19**
Place Ho. Cl. PO15: Fare . . . 2E **25**
Plaitford Gro. PO9: Hav . . . 5B **20**
Planet Ice
Gosport . . . **4E 39**
Playfair Rd. PO5: S'sea . . . 5H **5** (3D **50**)
Pleasant Rd. PO4: S'sea . . . 3H **51**
Plover Cl. PO14: Stub . . . 3D **36**
Plover Reach PO4: S'sea . . . 2H **51**
Plovers Rd. PO8: Horn . . . 6A **6**
Plumley Wlk. PO9: Hav . . . 2D **20**
Plumpton Gdns. PO3: Ports . . . 2D **42**
Plumpton Gro. PO7: W'lle . . . 6B **10**
Plymouth Dr. PO14: Stub . . . 3C **36**
Plymouth St. PO5: S'sea . . . 4G **5** (3C **50**)
Poinsettia Cl. PO15: Seg . . . 6A **12**
Polo Ct. GU32: Pet . . . 4D **56**
The Pompey Cen. . . . 2F **51**
Pond La. PO8: Clan . . . 1F **7**
Pond Piece PO7: Den . . . 4B **8**
Ponsonby Ho. PO5: S'sea . . . 4G **5** (3C **50**)
Pook La. PO9: Warb . . . 4G **33**
(not continuous)
PO17: Fare . . . 5B **14**
Popham Ct. PO9: Hav . . . 3C **20**
Poplar Dr. PO14: Fare . . . 3G **25**
Poplar Gro. PO11: H Isl . . . 3C **54**

80 A-Z Portsmouth

Raglan Ct.—Rowland Rd.

Raglan Ct. PO12: Gos 3C 48
Raglan St. PO5: S'sea 3H 5 (2D 50)
Raglan Ter. PO10: Ems 2E 35
Rails La. PO11: H Isl 5D 54
Railway Cotts. PO6: Cosh 6D 30
Railway Triangle Ind. Est.
PO6: Farl 5D 30
Railway Vw. PO1: Ports 2H 5 (2D 50)
Raleigh Ho. PO1: Ports 3C 4
Ralph Rd. PO6: Cosh 3C 28
Rambler Dr. PO13: Gos 1G 47
Ramblers Way PO7: W'lle 6B 10
Ramillies PO1: Ports 1C 4
Ramillies Ho. *PO12: Gos 3E 49*
(off The Anchorage)
PO14: Fare 4G 25
Rampart Gdns. PO3: Ports 6B 30
Rampart Row PO12: Gos 4G 49
Ramsay Pl. PO13: Gos 3C 38
Ramscote GU31: Pet 3E 57
Ramsdale Av. PO9: Hav 4C 20
Ramsey Rd. PO11: H Isl 4C 54
Ramshill GU31: Pet 3E 57
Rams Wlk. GU32: Pet 4D 56
Randal Vw. *PO14: Fare 4G 25*
(in Broadlaw Walk Shop. Cen.)
Randolph Rd. PO2: Ports 2A 42
Ranelagh Rd. PO2: Ports 4G 41
PO9: Hav 2D 32
Range Grn. PO2: Ports 2G 41
Rannoch Cl. PO15: Fare 6G 13
Ransome Cl. PO14: Titch 4B 24
Ranvilles La. PO14: Fare, Stub 3D 24
Rapley Ct. *PO11: H Isl 4A 54*
(off Stamford Av.)
Rapson Cl. PO6: Cosh 2G 29
Ratsey La. PO1: Ports 1E 51
Raven Cl. PO13: Gos 1G 47
Ravens Cl. PO14: Stub 3F 37
Ravenswood Gdns. PO5: S'sea 5D 50
RAVENSWOOD HOUSE 1G 13
Rawlinson Ter. PO1: Ports 1C 4 (1A 50)
Ray Cl. GU31: Pet 2E 57
Raymond Rd. PO6: Cosh 2C 28
Raynes Rd. PO13: Lee S 3D 46
Reading Ho. PO11: H Isl 5B 54
Readon Cl. GU31: Pet 3E 57
Readon Ho. GU31: Pet 3E 57
Record Rd. PO10: Ems 2C 34
Rectory Av. PO6: Farl 2H 31
Rectory Cl. PO12: Gos 5C 48
PO14: Stub 2E 37
Rectory Rd. PO9: Langs 3F 33
(not continuous)
The Redan PO12: Gos 6E 49
Red Barn Av. PO16: Portc 2A 28
Red Barn La. PO15: Fare 5G 13
PO16: Fare 5G 13
Redbridge Gro. PO9: Bed 6D 20
Redcar Av. PO3: Ports 4C 42
Redcliffe Gdns. PO4: S'sea 6E 51
RED HILL 6H 11
Redhill Ho. PO1: Ports 1D 50
Redhill Rd. PO9: R Cas 1H 21
Redhouse Pk. Gdns. PO12: Gos 1A 48
Redlands Gro. PO4: S'sea 3A 52
Redlands La. PO10: Ems 5D 22
PO14: Fare 2H 25
PO16: Fare 2H 25
Redlea Ct. PO12: Gos 1A 48
Redlynch Cl. PO9: Hav 5H 21
Redmill Dr. PO13: Lee S 6H 37
Rednal Ho. PO5: S'sea 3H 5 (2D 50)
Redoubt Ct. PO14: Fare 5H 25
Redpoll Rd. PO7: W'lle 6E 9
Redshank Rd. PO8: Horn 6A 6
Redwing Ct. PO4: S'sea 2A 52
PO10: Ems 5E 23
Redwing Rd. PO8: Clan 1C 6
Redwood Ct. PO7: W'lle 1G 19
Redwood Dr. PO16: Portc 3H 27
Redwood Gro. PO9: Hav 5G 21
Redwood Lodge PO16: Fare 1B 26
Reedling Dr. PO4: S'sea 2A 52
Reedmace Cl. PO7: W'lle 3A 20
Reed's Pl. PO12: Gos 2C 48
Reeds Rd. PO12: Gos 6H 39
Reed Way GU32: Pet 6B 56
Reel Cinema
Fareham 2B 26
Rees Hall PO5: S'sea 6E 5
Reeves Dr. GU31: Pet 6C 56
Regal Cl. PO6: Cosh 3B 30
Regency Ct. PO1: Ports 5B 4 (3A 50)
Regency Gdns. PO7: W'lle 3F 19
Regency Pl. PO15: Fare 2G 25
Regent Ct. PO1: Ports 6H 41
Regent Pl. PO5: S'sea 4B 50
Regents Ct. PO9: Langs 3F 33
PO17: K Vil 2G 13
Regents M. GU32: Pet 3B 56
Regents Pl. PO12: Gos 1F 49
Regents Trade Pk. PO13: Gos 6C 26
Reginald Rd. PO4: S'sea 4G 51
Reigate Ho. PO1: Ports 1D 50
Relay Rd. PO7: W'lle 1F 19
The Reldas *PO1: Ports 6B 4*
(off Oyster St.)
Relf Cl. PO15: Fare 6F 13
Renny Rd. PO1: Ports 2E 51
Renown Gdns. PO8: Cowp 2H 9
Renown Ho. *PO12: Gos 3E 49*
(off The Anchorage)
Repton Cl. PO12: Gos 3A 48
Reservoir La. GU32: Pet 2D 56
Resolution Ho. *PO12: Gos 3E 49*
(off The Anchorage)
Rest-a-Wyle Av. PO11: H Isl 2C 54
The Retreat PO5: S'sea 6G 5 (4C 50)
PO10: S'brne 3H 35
The Retreat Holiday Cvn. Pk. 5G 55
Revenge Cl. PO4: S'sea 1A 52
Revenge Ho. PO12: Gos 3E 49
Reynolds Rd. PO12: Gos 5E 49
Rhinefield Cl. PO9: Hav 5C 20
Rhys Ct. PO4: S'sea 3G 51
Ribble Gdns. PO16: Portc 3G 27
Richard Ct. PO3: Ports 1G 51
Richard Gro. PO12: Gos 4G 39
Richardson Dr. PO15: Fare 1F 25
Riches M. PO16: Fare 2A 26
Richmond PO1: Ports 1B 4
Richmond Cl. PO11: H Isl 3H 53
Richmond Dr. PO11: H Isl 3H 53
Richmond Gdns. *PO7: Purb 4E 19*
(off Crofton Cl.)
Richmond Pl. PO1: Ports 3D 4 (2B 50)
PO5: S'sea 5C 50
Richmond Ri. PO16: Portc 2A 28
Richmond Rd. PO5: S'sea 5D 50
PO12: Gos 3C 48
PO13: Lee S 6F 37
Richmond Ter. *PO5: S'sea 5C 50*
(off Netley Rd.)
Riders La. PO9: Hav 5E 21
(not continuous)
Ridge Cl. PO8: Clan 1C 6
RIDGE COMMON 1A 56
Ridge Comn. La. GU32: Ste, Stro 2A 56
The Ridgeway PO16: Fare 2E 27
Ridgeway Cl. PO6: Cosh 2D 28
Ridgeway Office Pk. GU32: Pet 5B 56
Ridgway PO9: Hav 2D 32
The Ridings PO2: Ports 1B 42
Rimington Rd. PO8: Cowp 4G 9
Ringwood Ho. PO9: Hav 4F 21
Ringwood Rd. PO4: S'sea 4H 51
Ripley Gro. PO3: Ports 5C 42
Ripon Ct. PO13: Gos 2H 47
Ripon Gdns. PO7: W'lle 6B 10
The Rise PO7: Wid 1F 31
Ritchie Cl. PO11: H Isl 4C 54
Rival Moor Rd. GU31: Pet 4G 57
Riverdale Av. PO7: W'lle 2A 20
River End PO7: Den 4B 8
Riverhead Cl. PO4: S'sea 2H 51
River La. PO15: F'ley 3E 13
Rivermead Ct. PO10: Ems 6E 23
Riversdale Gdns. PO9: Hav 1F 33
Riverside Av. PO16: Fare 6D 14
Riverside M. PO17: Wick 2A 14
Riverside Ter. PO10: Ems 3E 35
Riverside Wlk. GU31: Pet 4E 57
(not continuous)
River's St. PO5: S'sea 4H 5 (3D 50)
Rivers St. PO7: Purb 4E 19
River St. PO10: Westb 5F 23
River Way PO9: Hav 6G 21
Roads Hill PO8: Cath 4A 6
Road Vw. PO2: Ports 5G 41
Robert Mack Ct. PO1: Ports 3C 4 (2B 50)
Roberts Cl. PO17: Wick 1A 14
Roberts Rd. PO12: Gos 1B 48
Robin Gdns. PO8: Cowp 3F 9
Robinia Cl. PO7: W'lle 2A 20
Robins Cl. PO14: Stub 2E 37
Robinson Ct. PO13: Lee S 2C 46
PO16: Portc 2A 28
Robinson Rd. PO14: Stub 4D 36
Robinson Way PO3: Ports 3E 43
Rochester Rd. PO4: S'sea 4F 51
Rochford Rd. PO6: Cosh 3H 29
Rockbourne Cl. PO9: Hav 5C 20
Rockingham Way PO16: Portc 3H 27
Rockrose Way PO6: Cosh 1E 29
Rockville Dr. PO7: W'lle 2G 19
Rockwood Ct. PO10: Ems 2D 34
Rodney Cl. PO13: Gos 6C 38
Rodney Ho. PO12: Gos 3F 49
Rodney Rd. PO4: S'sea 2F 51
Rodney Way PO8: Horn 1B 10
Roebuck Av. PO15: F'ley 3F 13
Roebuck Cl. PO6: Cosh 4B 30
Roebuck Dr. PO12: Gos 6A 40
Roedeer Cl. PO10: Ems 5E 23
Rogate Gdns. PO16: Portc 2A 28
Rogate Ho. PO1: Ports 1H 5 (1D 50)
Rogers Cl. PO12: Gos 1D 48
Rogers Mead PO11: H Isl 2B 44
Roko Health Club
Portsmouth 2C 42
Roland Cl. PO8: Horn 1B 10
Roman Ct. PO10: S'brne 2H 35
Roman Grn. PO7: Den 3A 8
Roman Gro. PO16: Portc 5B 28
Roman Way PO9: Bed 1C 32
Romsey Av. PO3: Ports 1H 51
PO16: Portc 3G 27
Romsey Rd. PO8: Horn 3C 6
Romyns Ct. PO14: Fare 2H 25
Rooke Ho. PO1: Ports 2C 4
The Rookery PO10: S'brne 2E 35
Rookery Av. PO15: White 2A 12
Rookes Cl. PO8: Horn 1B 10
Rookes M. GU31: Pet 3E 57
Rook Farm Way PO11: H Isl 3B 54
Rooksbury Cft. PO9: Hav 4G 21
Rooksway Gro. PO16: Portc 3F 27
Rookwood Vw. PO7: Den 2B 8
Rope Quays PO12: Gos 2F 49
The Rope Wlk. PO16: Fare 3B 26
Ropley Rd. PO9: Hav 4H 21
Rosebay Ct. PO7: W'lle 4H 19
Rosebery Av. PO6: Cosh 4C 30
Rosecott PO8: Horn 6D 6
Rose Ct. PO12: Gos 1C 48
Rosedale Cl. PO14: Titch 3B 24
Rose Hill PO8: Cowp 1A 10
Roselands PO8: Horn 2A 10
Rosemary Gdns. PO15: White 1A 12
Rosemary La. PO1: Ports 3B 4 (2A 50)
PO7: W'lle 2F 19
Rosemary Wlk. PO13: Lee S 1D 46
Rosemary Way PO8: Horn 3B 10
The Rosery PO12: Gos 6D 48
Rose Twr. PO5: S'sea 6D 50
Rosetta Rd. PO4: S'sea 3H 51
Rosewood PO13: Gos 4E 39
Rosewood Gdns. PO8: Clan 2G 7
Rosina Cl. PO7: W'lle 1B 20
Roslyn Ho. PO5: S'sea 6G 5 (4C 50)
Ross Ho. PO13: Lee S 6F 37
Ross Way PO13: Lee S 6H 37
Rostrevor La. PO4: S'sea 6E 51
Rostrevor Mans. PO4: S'sea 6E 51
Rotherbrook Ct. GU32: Pet 5B 56
Rother Cl. GU31: Pet 3G 57
Rotherwick Cl. PO9: Hav 4H 21
Rothesay Rd. PO12: Gos 6G 39
Rothwell Cl. PO6: Cosh 2E 29
The Round Ho. PO1: Ports 4B 4 (3A 50)
Roundhouse Ct. PO11: H Isl 5D 54
Roundhouse Mdw. PO10: S'brne 4E 35
The Round Tower 6A 4 (4H 49)
Roundway PO7: W'lle 1H 19
Rowallan Av. PO13: Gos 5C 38
Rowan Av. PO8: Cowp 5B 10
Rowan Cl. PO13: Lee S 2D 46
Rowan Ct. PO4: S'sea 3F 51
Rowan Rd. PO9: Hav 6H 21
ROWANS HOSPICE 5D 18
Rowan Way PO14: Fare 3D 24
Rowbury Rd. PO9: Hav 3D 20
Rowena Ct. *PO5: S'sea 4D 50*
(off Outram Rd.)
Rowes All. 5A 4
Rowin Cl. PO11: H Isl 5F 55
Rowland Rd. PO6: Cosh 2C 28
PO15: Fare 1H 25

82 A-Z Portsmouth

Rowlands Av.—Sandford Av.

Rowlands Av. PO7: W'lle 6G 9
ROWLANDS CASTLE 5H 11
Rowlands Castle Golf Course 5H 11
Rowlands Castle Rd. PO8: Horn, Ids 1D 10
Rowlands Sq. GU32: Pet 5C 56
ROWNER 4C 38
Rowner Cl. PO13: Gos 4C 38
Rowner La. PO13: Gos 3C 38
Rowner Rd. PO13: Gos 3A 38
(not continuous)
Rowner Swimming Cen. 1G 47
Rowner Wlk. PO13: Gos 5C 38
(not continuous)
Rownhams Rd. PO9: Hav 4D 20
Row Wood La. PO13: Gos 4B 38
The Royal PO11: H Isl 5A 54
Royal Albert Wlk. PO4: S'sea 5E 51
Royal Clarence Yd. PO12: Gos 1F 49
Royal Gdns. PO9: R Cas 6G 11
Royal Garrison Church 6C 4 (4A 50)
Royal Ga. PO4: S'sea 5H 51
Royal Haslar Development 5F 49
Royal Military Police Mus. 3E 17
Royal Naval Cotts. PO17: S'wick 3D 16
Royal Navy Submarine Mus. 4G 49
Royal Oak Ct. PO1: Ports 2D 4
PO14: Fare 3H 25
Royal Sovereign Av. PO14: Fare 6A 26
Royal Way PO7: W'lle 2A 20
Rudgwick Cl. PO16: Portc 3H 27
Rudmore Ct. PO2: Ports 4G 41
Rudmore Rd. PO2: Ports 5G 41
RUDMORE RDBT. 5H 41
Rudmore Sq. PO2: Ports 5G 41
Rudolph Ct. PO7: Purb 4E 19
Rugby Rd. PO5: S'sea 3E 51
Runnymede PO15: Fare 5F 13
Rushes Ct. PO7: W'lle 6H 9
Rushes Farm GU32: Pet 3C 56
Rushes Rd. GU32: Pet 3C 56
Rushmere Wlk. PO9: Hav 3D 20
Ruskin Rd. PO4: S'sea 3G 51
Ruskin Way PO8: Cowp 3H 9
Russell Churcher Ct. PO12: Gos 6F 39
Russell Cl. PO13: Lee S 1D 46
Russell Pl. PO16: Fare 2A 26
Russell Rd. PO9: Hav 6F 21
PO13: Lee S 2D 46
Russell St. PO12: Gos 1C 48
Russell Way GU31: Pet 5E 57
Russet Gdns. PO10: S'brne 3F 35
Russett La. PO7: W'lle 2F 19
Rustington Ho. PO1: Ports 2G 5
Rutherford Ho. PO12: Gos 6B 40
Rydal Cl. PO6: Cosh 2F 29
Rydal Ho. PO6: Cosh 2F 29
Rydal Rd. PO12: Gos 5G 39
Ryde Pl. PO13: Lee S 3E 47
Ryecroft PO9: Warb 2H 33
Ryefield Cl. GU31: Pet 4G 57

S

Sackville St. PO5: S'sea 5F 5 (3C 50)
(not continuous)
Saddleback Rd. PO7: W'lle 6E 9
Sadlers Wlk. PO10: S'brne 3E 35
Saffron Way PO15: White 2A 12
Sage Cl. PO7: W'lle 3A 20
Sainsbury Lodge *PO1: Ports 2E 51*
(off Lucknow St.)
St Agathas Way PO1: Ports 1F 5 (1C 50)
St Alban's Rd. PO4: S'sea 4F 51
PO9: Hav 5G 21
St Andrew Cl. PO8: Horn 3C 6
St Andrews Ct. PO1: Ports 4E 5 (3B 50)
St Andrew's Rd. PO5: S'sea 6H 5 (4D 50)
PO6: Farl 3H 31
PO11: H Isl 5D 54
PO12: Gos 3D 48
St Anne's Gro. PO14: Fare 4H 25
St Ann's Cres. PO12: Gos 1C 48
St Ann's Rd. PO4: S'sea 4F 51
PO8: Horn 6C 6
St Aubin's Pk. PO11: H Isl 4H 53
St Augustine Rd. PO4: S'sea 5F 51
St Barbara Way PO2: Ports 1B 42
St Bartholomew's Gdns.
PO5: S'sea 6H 5 (4D 50)
St Benedict Rd. PO11: H Isl 4D 54
St Catherines Ct. PO11: H Isl 4G 53
St Catherine's Rd. PO11: H Isl 4G 53
St Catherine St. PO5: S'sea 6D 50
St Catherines Way PO16: Fare 2E 27
St Chad's Av. PO2: Ports 3A 42
St Christopher Av. PO16: Fare 6B 14
St Christophers Gdns. PO13: Gos 3C 38
St Christophers Rd. PO9: Bed 5C 20
St Clares Av. PO9: Hav 2D 20
St Clares Ct. PO9: Hav 3D 20
St Colman's Av. PO6: Cosh 3C 30
St Davids Ct. PO13: Gos 1G 47
St David's Rd. PO5: S'sea 5H 5 (3D 50)
PO8: Clan 2G 7
St Denys Wlk. PO9: Hav 3D 20
St Edward's Rd. PO12: Gos 3D 48
St Edwards Rd. PO5: S'sea 6F 5 (4C 50)
St Edwards Ter. PO12: Gos 1C 48
St Faith's Cl. PO12: Gos 2C 48
St Faiths Ho. PO1: Ports 1H 5
St Faith's Rd. PO1: Ports 1H 5 (1D 50)
St Francis Ct. PO2: Ports 1A 42
St Francis Pl. PO9: Hav 6E 21
St Francis Rd. PO12: Gos 6E 49
St Georges Av. PO9: Warb 2H 33
St George's Bus. Cen. PO1: Ports 3C 4 (2A 50)
St George's Ct. PO5: S'sea 6E 5 (4B 50)
PO16: Fare 3B 26
St George's Ind. Est. PO4: S'sea 2G 51
St George's Rd. PO1: Ports 4C 4 (3A 50)
PO4: S'sea 5G 51
PO6: Cosh 3B 30
PO11: H Isl 4H 53
St Georges Rd. PO7: Den 2A 8
St George's Sq. PO1: Ports 3C 4 (2A 50)
St George's Wlk. *PO7: W'lle 2G 19*
(off Hambledon Rd.)
St Georges Wlk. PO12: Gos 2F 49
St George's Way PO1: Ports 3C 4 (2A 50)
St Giles Way PO8: Horn 3C 6
St Helena Way PO16: Portc 3A 28
St Helen's Cl. PO4: S'sea 5F 51
St Helen's Ct. *PO4: S'sea 6E 51*
(off St Helen's Pde.)
St Helens Ho. PO14: Fare 3E 25
St Helens Mans. *PO4: S'sea 6E 51*
(off St Helen's Pde.)
St Helen's Pde. PO4: S'sea 6E 51
St Helen's Rd. PO11: H Isl 4H 53
St Helens Rd. PO12: Gos 4A 48
St Helier Rd. PO12: Gos 5A 40
St Hellen's Rd. PO6: Dray 3F 31
St Herman's Cvn. Est. 5E 55
St Herman's Rd. PO11: H Isl 5E 55
St Hilda Av. PO8: Horn 3C 6
St Hubert Rd. PO8: Horn 3C 6
St James Cl. PO8: Clan 1C 6
St James Ct. PO5: S'sea 5B 50
ST JAMES HOSPITAL 2A 52
St James Pl. PO4: S'sea 2H 51
St James' Rd. PO10: Ems 2D 34
St James's Rd. PO5: S'sea 5F 5 (3C 50)
St James's St. PO1: Ports 2D 4 (2B 50)
St James Way PO16: Portc 3A 28
St Jaques Way PO7: Den 2A 8
St John's Av. PO7: Purb 5G 19
St John's Cl. PO12: Gos 2D 48
St Johns Cl. PO11: H Isl 4A 54
St John's Ct. PO2: Ports 4G 41
St Johns M. PO5: S'sea 6H 5 (4D 50)
St John's Rd. PO6: Cosh 3B 30
PO9: Bed 5C 20
PO10: S'brne 2H 35
St John's Sq. PO12: Gos 2D 48
St John the Evangelist Roman Catholic Cathedral 2E 5 (2B 50)
St Judes Cl. PO5: S'sea 4C 50
St Juliens Ho. PO14: Fare 4H 25
St Kitts Ho. PO6: Cosh 1D 28
St Leonard's Av. PO11: H Isl 3C 54
St Leonards Cl. PO15: Seg 6A 12
St Lucia Ho. PO6: Cosh 1D 28
St Luke's Community Sports Cen. 3G 5 (2C 50)
St Lukes Rd. PO12: Gos 1C 48
St Margarets La. PO14: Titch 2A 24
St Margaret's Rd. PO11: H Isl 4C 54
St Mark's Cl. PO12: Gos 6D 48
St Marks Ct. PO12: Gos 2C 48
St Mark's Pl. PO12: Gos 5D 48
St Mark's Rd. PO2: Ports 4H 41
PO12: Gos 6C 48
St Martin's Ho. PO5: S'sea 6D 50
St Mary's Av. PO12: Gos 5C 48
ST MARY'S HOSPITAL 2G 51
St Mary's Ho. PO3: Ports 1F 51
ST MARY'S NHS TREATMENT CENTRE 2G 51
St Mary's Rd. PO1: Ports 1E 51
PO3: Ports 1E 51
PO11: H Isl 4B 54
PO14: Stub 1E 37
St Matthew's Ct. PO12: Gos 2F 49
St Matthew's Rd. PO6: Cosh 3B 30
St Michaels Ct. PO6: Cosh 2F 29
St Michael's Gro. PO14: Fare 4H 25
St Michael's Ho. PO14: Fare 3H 25
St Michaels Pl. PO7: W'lle 1H 19
St Michael's Rd. PO1: Ports 4E 5 (3B 50)
PO9: Bed 5C 20
St Michaels Way PO8: Horn 3C 6
St Nicholas Av. PO13: Gos 5B 38
St Nicholas Rd. PO9: Bed 6C 20
St Nicholas Row PO17: Wick 2A 14
St Nicholas St. PO1: Ports 6C 4 (4A 50)
St Omers Ho. PO5: S'sea 6G 5
St Paul's Rd. PO5: S'sea 5E 5 (3B 50)
St Paul's Sq. PO5: S'sea 5E 5 (3B 50)
St Peter's Av. PO11: H Isl 3E 45
St Peters Cl. PO7: W'lle 1H 19
St Peter's Ct. *GU32: Pet 4D 56*
(off Hylton Rd.)
St Peters Ct. *PO10: Ems 3E 35*
(off High St.)
St Peters Gro. PO5: S'sea 6H 5 (4D 50)
St Peter's Rd. PO11: H Isl 1E 45
St Peters Rd. GU31: Pet 4D 56
GU32: Pet 4D 56
St Peter's Sq. PO10: Ems 3D 34
St Peters Way PO7: W'lle 1H 19
St Piran's Av. PO3: Ports 6C 42
St Quentin Ho. *PO14: Fare 4G 25*
(off Bishopsfield Rd.)
St Richards Gdns. *PO7: Purb 4E 19*
(off Campbell Cres.)
St Ronan's Av. PO4: S'sea 5E 51
St Ronan's Rd. PO4: S'sea 6E 51
St Sebastian Cres. PO16: Fare 6B 14
St Simon's Rd. PO5: S'sea 5D 50
St Stephen's Rd. PO2: Ports 5A 42
St Swithun's Rd. PO2: Ports 3B 42
St Theresa's Cl. PO9: Bed 6C 20
St Thomas Av. PO11: H Isl 4H 53
St Thomas Cl. PO16: Fare 6C 14
St Thomas's Ct. PO1: Ports 5C 4 (3A 50)
St Thomas's Rd. PO12: Gos 5H 39
St Thomas's St. PO1: Ports 6B 4 (4A 50)
St Ursula Gro. PO5: S'sea 6H 5 (4D 50)
St Valerie Rd. PO12: Gos 4D 48
St Vincent Cres. PO8: Horn 1B 10
St Vincent Leisure Cen. 1E 49
St Vincent Rd. PO5: S'sea 5D 50
PO12: Gos 1D 48
St Vincents Ho. PO16: Fare 2F 27
St Vincent St. PO5: S'sea 4E 5 (3C 50)
Salcombe Av. PO3: Ports 4C 42
Salerno Dr. PO12: Gos 3B 48
Salerno Ho. PO14: Fare 4H 25
Salerno Rd. PO2: Ports 1H 41
Salet Way PO7: W'lle 6B 10
Salisbury Rd. PO4: S'sea 5F 51
PO6: Cosh 4C 30
Salisbury Ter. PO13: Lee S 2D 46
Salterns Av. PO4: S'sea 2H 51
Salterns Cl. PO11: H Isl 4E 55
Salterns Est. PO16: Fare 4B 26
Salterns La. PO11: H Isl 4D 54
PO16: Fare 4B 26
Saltern's Rd. PO13: Lee S 5D 36
PO14: Stub 5D 36
The Salthouse Apts. *PO12: Gos 1F 49*
(off Salt Meat La.)
The Saltings PO6: Farl 4G 31
PO9: Langs 5F 33
Saltmarsh La. PO11: H Isl 2A 54
Salt Meat La. PO12: Gos 1F 49
Salvia Cl. PO7: W'lle 3A 20
Sampson Rd. PO1: Ports 1A 4 (1H 49)
PO14: Fare 5H 25
Samson Cl. PO13: Gos 6D 38
Samuel Mortimer Cl. PO15: Fare 2D 24
Samuel Rd. PO1: Ports 1F 51
Sandalwood Cl. PO8: Clan 2G 7
Sandcroft Cl. PO12: Gos 4A 48
Sanderling Lodge PO12: Gos 2F 49
Sanderling Rd. PO4: S'sea 2A 52
The Sanderlings PO11: H Isl 5C 54
The Sanderson Cen. PO12: Gos 2D 48
Sandford Av. PO12: Gos 3H 47

Upper Piece—Welchwood Cl.

Upper Piece PO7: Den 4C 8
Up. St Michael's Gro. PO14: Fare 3H 25
Upper Wardown GU31: Pet 3F 57
Upper Wharf PO16: Fare 3C 26
Upton Cl. PO9: Hav 2D 20
Usborne Cl. PO13: Lee S 6H 37

V

Vadne Gdns. PO12: Gos 1D 48
The Vale PO5: S'sea 5C 50
PO8: Horn 4C 6
Vale Gro. PO12: Gos 6G 39
Valentine Cl. PO15: Fare 6E 13
Valentine Ct. PO7: W'lle 1A 20
Valerian Av. PO15: Titch 6B 12
Valetta Pk. PO10: Ems 3C 34
Valiant Gdns. PO2: Ports 1H 41
Valley Cl. PO7: Wid 6E 19
Valley Pk. Dr. PO8: Clan 1D 6
Valsheba Dr. PO14: Stub 4D 36
Vancouver Av. PO7: Purb 5G 19
Vanguard Ct. PO4: S'sea 4B 52
Vanguard Ho. PO2: Ports 5H 41
Vanguard Rd. PO12: Gos 5A 40
Vannes Pde. *PO16: Fare 2B 26*
(off Harper Way)
Vanstone Rd. PO13: Gos 5D 38
Varos Cl. PO12: Gos 1C 48
Vauxhall Way GU32: Pet 4C 56
Vectis Rd. PO12: Gos 4A 48
Vectis Way PO6: Cosh 4B 30
Velder Av. PO4: S'sea 2G 51
Venerable Rd. PO14: Fare 6A 26
Vengeance Rd. PO13: Lee S 6G 37
Venice Cl. PO7: W'lle 1A 20
Ventnor Rd. PO4: S'sea 3E 51
PO13: Gos 2B 38
Ventnor Way PO16: Fare 2E 27
Venture Ct. PO3: Ports 6C 30
Venture Ind. Pk. PO3: Ports 6C 30
PO13: Gos 2D 38
Venture Sidings PO4: S'sea 2F 51
Verbena Cres. PO8: Cowp, Horn 3B 10
Vernon Av. PO4: S'sea 2G 51
(not continuous)
Vernon Cl. PO12: Gos 2C 48
Vernon Ct. PO2: Ports 3A 42
Vernon M. PO4: S'sea 2G 51
Vernon Rd. PO3: Ports 3C 42
PO12: Gos 2C 48
Verwood Rd. PO9: Hav 3H 21
Veryan PO14: Fare 2G 25
Vian Cl. PO13: Gos 1C 38
Vian Rd. PO7: W'lle 3F 19
Vicarage Ct. PO16: Fare 1B 26
Vicarage La. PO14: Stub 2E 37
Vicarage Ter. PO12: Gos 5F 39
Victoria Av. PO1: Ports 6D 4 (4B 50)
PO7: Wid 6D 18
PO11: H Isl 4B 54
Victoria Ct. PO11: H Isl 4A 54
Victoria Gro. PO5: S'sea 6H 5 (4D 50)
Victoria M. PO17: K Vil 2G 13
Victoria Pl. PO12: Gos 3D 48
Victoria Rd. PO1: Ports 1H 49
PO7: W'lle 2G 19
PO10: Ems 2C 34
PO11: H Isl 3B 44
Victoria Rd. Nth. PO5: S'sea 6H 5 (4D 50)
Victoria Rd. Sth. PO5: S'sea 6H 5 (5D 50)
Victoria Spur PO1: Ports 4B 50
Victoria Sq. PO13: Lee S 1C 46
Victoria St. PO1: Ports 6G 41
PO12: Gos 2E 49
Victoria Ter. PO6: Cosh 4B 30
PO10: Ems 2E 35
PO10: S'brne 3G 35
Victor Rd. PO3: Ports 6B 42
Victory Av. PO8: Horn 1A 10
Victory Bus. Cen. *PO1: Ports 2E 51*
(off Somers Rd. Nth.)
Victory Ct. PO7: W'lle 1G 19
PO13: Gos 4D 38
PO13: Lee S 1C 46
Victory Gate 2A 4 (2H 49)
Victory Grn. PO2: Ports 3G 41
Victory Ho. PO6: P Sol 4E 29
Victory Indoor Bowls Club 2H 41
Victory Rd. PO1: Ports 3B 4 (2A 50)
PO14: Stub 3F 37
Victory Trad. Est. PO3: Ports 3C 42
Viking Cl. PO14: Stub 2D 36
Viking Ct. PO1: Ports 2H 5
Viking Way PO8: Horn 2C 6
Villa Gdns. PO7: W'lle 1G 19
Village Cl. PO14: Stub 3E 37
Village Ga. PO14: Titch 2B 24
Village Rd. PO12: Gos 5B 48
Village St. GU32: Pet 1F 57
Ville De Paris Rd. PO14: Fare 6A 26
Villiers Ct. *PO5: S'sea 5C 50*
(off Palmerston Rd.)
Villiers Rd. PO5: S'sea 5C 50
(not continuous)
Vimy Ho. PO14: Fare 3G 25
Vincent Gro. PO16: Portc 4A 28
Vine Coppice PO7: W'lle 5G 19
Vineside PO13: Gos 4E 39
Violet Av. PO14: Stub 3D 36
Violet Ct. PO7: W'lle 5E 9
Virginia Pk. Rd. PO12: Gos 1B 48
Vision Pk. GU32: Pet 4B 56
Vista PO4: S'sea 3F 51
Vita Rd. PO2: Ports 2A 42
Vivash Rd. PO1: Ports 2E 51
Vixen Cl. PO14: Stub 3D 36
Voyager Pk. PO3: Ports 3C 42
Voyager Pk. Nth. PO3: Ports 2C 42
Vue Cinema
Portsmouth 4A 4
The Vulcan PO1: Ports 4B 4 (3A 50)
Vulcan Way PO13: Lee S 4H 37

W

Wade Ct. Rd. PO9: Hav 3G 33
Wade La. PO9: Hav 4G 33
Waders Wlk. PO11: H Isl 3C 54
Wadham Rd. PO2: Ports 3H 41
Wagtail Rd. PO8: Horn 6A 6
Wagtail Way PO16: Portc 3F 27
Wainscott Rd. PO4: S'sea 5G 51
Wainwright Cl. PO6: Dray 5E 31
Wait End Rd. PO7: W'lle 3G 19
Waitland Cl. PO7: W'lle 3F 19
Wakefield Av. PO16: Fare 6H 13
Wakefield Ct. PO7: Purb 6H 19
Wakefield Pl. *PO12: Gos 5C 48*
(off Stephenson Cl.)
Wakefords Way PO9: Hav 3G 21
Wake Lawn PO4: S'sea 4A 52
Walberant Bldgs. PO3: Ports 1B 42
Walberton Av. PO6: Cosh 3C 30
Walberton Ct. PO6: Cosh 3C 30
Walburton Way PO8: Clan 1D 6
Walden Gdns. PO8: Horn 6B 6
Walden Rd. PO2: Ports 3G 41
Walford Rd. PO6: Cosh 2G 29
Walker Pl. PO13: Gos 4D 38
Walker Rd. PO2: Ports 3G 41
Wallace Rd. PO2: Ports 5B 42
WALLINGTON 1D 26
Wallington Ct. PO14: Fare 4H 25
PO16: Fare 6D 14
Wallington Hill PO16: Fare 1C 26
Wallington Orchard PO16: Fare 6D 14
Wallington Rd. PO2: Ports 4B 42
Wallington Shore Rd. PO16: Fare 2D 26
(Cams Hill)
PO16: Fare 1C 26
(North Wallington)
Wallington Way PO16: Fare 1C 26
Wallisdean Av. PO3: Ports 6D 42
PO14: Fare 3H 25
Wallis Gdns. PO7: W'lle 6G 9
Wallis Rd. PO7: W'lle 6G 9
Wallrock Wlk. PO10: Ems 5D 22
Walmer Rd. PO1: Ports 2E 51
Walnut Dr. PO14: Stub 3D 36
Walnut Tree Cl. PO11: H Isl 4B 54
Walnut Tree Dr. PO10: W'cote 6H 23
Walpole Rd. PO12: Gos 3F 49
Walpole Ter. PO12: Gos 4D 48
Walsall Rd. PO3: Ports 1G 51
Walsingham Cl. PO6: Cosh 2H 29
Waltham Cl. PO16: Portc 1A 28
Waltham St. PO5: S'sea 4E 5 (3B 50)
Walton Cl. PO7: W'lle 4G 19
PO12: Gos 3C 48
Walton Ct. PO1: Ports 5C 4
PO15: Fare 5F 13
Walton Rd. PO6: Farl 5D 30
PO12: Gos 3C 48
Walton Rd. Ind. Est. PO6: Farl 5E 31
Wandesford Pl. PO12: Gos 4G 39
Warbler Cl. PO8: Horn 6A 6
WARBLINGTON 2H 33
Warblington Av. PO9: Warb 2H 33
Warblington Ct. PO1: Ports 5C 4 (3A 50)
Warblington Pl. PO3: Ports 1G 51
Warblington Rd. PO10: Ems 4C 34
Warblington Station (Rail) 1H 33
Warblington St. PO1: Ports 5C 4 (3A 50)
Warblington Ter. PO9: Hav 2G 33
Warbrook Ct. PO9: Hav 4H 21
Ward Ct. PO11: H Isl 4A 54
Ward Cres. PO10: Ems 6E 23
Wardens Cl. PO11: H Isl 2B 54
Warders Ct. PO12: Gos 2D 48
Ward Ho. PO1: Ports 1C 4 (1B 50)
Ward Rd. PO4: S'sea 5G 51
Wardroom Rd. PO2: Ports 4F 41
Warfield Av. PO7: W'lle 2G 19
Warfield Cres. PO7: W'lle 2G 19
Warnborough Ct. PO9: Hav 3H 21
Warnford Cl. PO12: Gos 3B 48
Warnford Cres. PO9: Hav 4D 20
Warren Av. PO4: S'sea 2G 51
Warren Cl. PO11: H Isl 3G 53
WARREN PARK 3C 20
The Warrior Bus. Cen. PO6: Farl 4G 31
Warrior Ct. PO12: Gos 3G 49
Warrior Ho. PO1: Ports 2B 4
Warsash Cl. PO9: Hav 3E 21
Warsash Gro. PO13: Gos 3B 38
Warsash Rd. PO14: Titch, Titch C 3A 24
Warspite Cl. PO2: Ports 1H 41
Warwick Cl. PO13: Lee S 3E 47
Warwick Ct. *PO10: Ems 3D 34*
(off High St.)
Warwick Cres. PO5: S'sea 5G 5 (3C 50)
Warwick Way PO17: Wick 1A 14
Wasdale Cl. PO8: Horn 3C 6
Washbrook Rd. PO6: Cosh 3H 29
Washington Rd. PO2: Ports 5H 41
PO10: Ems 2D 34
Waterberry Dr. PO7: W'lle 6E 9
Watercress Ter. PO10: Ems 5E 23
Watergate PO12: Gos 3G 49
Waterlock Gdns. PO4: S'sea 3B 52
Waterloo Cl. PO8: Cowp 4F 9
Waterloo Rd. PO9: Hav 1F 33
PO12: Gos 6E 49
Waterloo St. PO5: S'sea 4F 5 (3C 50)
WATERLOOVILLE 2G 19
Waterlooville Golf Course 5B 10
Waterlooville Leisure Cen. 6E 9
Waterman Ter. *PO5: S'sea 4E 51*
(off Boulton Rd.)
Watermead Rd. PO6: Farl 4G 31
Watermill Ct. PO9: Hav 2F 33
The Waters PO17: F'ley 4G 13
Water's Edge PO13: Lee S 3D 46
Watersedge PO17: Wick 1A 14
Waters Edge Cvn. Pk. 5G 55
Watersedge Gdns. PO10: Ems 3D 34
Watersedge Rd. PO6: Cosh 3E 29
Waterside Gdns. PO7: W'lle 3E 19
PO16: Fare 1D 26
Waterside La. PO16: Portc 5C 28
Watersmeet PO16: Fare 4B 26
Waterworks Rd. GU32: Pet 1E 57
PO6: Farl 3F 31
Watts Rd. PO1: Ports 6H 41
Wavell Rd. PO13: Gos 2D 38
Waveney Cl. PO13: Lee S 1D 46
Waverley Gro. PO4: S'sea 5E 51
PO5: S'sea 5E 51
Waverley Path PO12: Gos 4A 48
Waverley Rd. PO5: S'sea 6D 50
PO6: Dray 3E 31
Wayfarer Cl. PO4: S'sea 2A 52
Wayfarers PO13: Gos 6D 38
Wayte St. PO6: Cosh 4B 30
Weavers Grn. PO9: Hav 6A 22
Webb Cl. PO11: H Isl 5C 54
Webbers Way PO12: Gos 5E 49
Webb La. PO11: H Isl 5C 54
Webb Rd. PO16: Portc 5B 28
WECOCK 3G 9
Wedgewood Cl. PO14: Stub 3E 37
Wedgwood Way PO8: Cowp 5G 9
Weevil La. PO12: Gos 1F 49
Welch Rd. PO4: S'sea 5E 51
PO12: Gos 6G 39
Welchwood Cl. PO8: Love 1H 9

88 A-Z Portsmouth

Well Copse Cl. PO8: Horn 4C 6
Weller Ho. PO1: Ports 6H 41
Wellesley Cl. PO7: W'lle 2G 19
Wellington Cl. PO8: Horn 1D 10
Wellington Ct. PO9: Hav 1F 33
  PO12: Gos 5A 40
Wellington Dr. PO13: Lee S 2E 47
Wellington Ga. PO7: W'lle 1F 19
Wellington Gro. PO16: Portc 4A 28
Wellington Retail Pk. 1G 19
Wellington St. PO5: S'sea 4F 5 (3C 50)
Wellington Ter. PO2: Ports 6A 42
  (off Hanway Rd.)
Wellington Way PO7: W'lle 2G 19
Well Mdw. PO9: Hav 3E 21
Wellow Cl. PO9: Bed 6D 20
Wells Cl. PO3: Ports 1H 51
Wellsworth La. PO9: Ids, R Cas 4H 11
Wembley Gro. PO6: Cosh 5C 30
Wendover Rd. PO9: Hav 1E 33
Wensley Gdns. PO10: Ems 6D 22
Wentworth Dr. PO8: Horn 6B 6
  PO10: S'brne 1H 35
Wesermarsch Rd. PO8: Cowp 3A 10
Wesley Ct. PO1: Ports 2E 51
Wesley Gro. PO3: Ports 2B 42
Wessex Cl. PO13: Lee S 1E 47
Wessex Ct. PO16: Fare 2B 26
Wessex Gdns. PO16: Portc 4H 27
Wessex Ga. PO8: Horn 1C 10
Wessex Rd. PO8: Horn 2C 6
W. Battery Rd. PO2: Ports 4F 41
Westborn Rd. PO16: Fare 2B 26
WESTBOURNE 6F 23
Westbourne Av. PO10: Ems 1D 34
Westbourne Cvn. Pk. 5H 23
Westbourne Cl. PO10: Ems 1E 35
Westbourne Ct. PO9: Hav 1E 33
Westbourne Rd. PO2: Ports 5B 42
  PO10: Ems, Westb 6E 23
The Westbrook Cen. 6B 10
Westbrooke Cl. PO8: Horn 1B 10
Westbrook Gro. PO7: Purb 4F 19
Westbrook Rd. PO16: Portc 5B 28
W. Bund Rd. PO6: P Sol 5F 29
Westbury Cl. PO6: Cosh 3C 48
Westbury Mall PO16: Fare 2B 26
Westbury Manor Mus. 2B 26
Westbury Rd. PO16: Fare 2B 26
Westbury Sq. PO16: Fare 2B 26
Westcliff Ct. PO13: Lee S 6H 37
West Ct. PO1: Ports 6A 42
  PO4: S'sea 4G 51
Westcroft Rd. PO12: Gos 2B 48
West Downs Cl. PO16: Fare 5A 14
WEST END 4G 25
Westerham Cl. PO6: Cosh 3A 30
Western Av. PO10: Ems 3B 34
Western Ct. PO16: Fare 2A 26
Western Pde. PO5: S'sea 4B 50
  PO10: Ems 4C 34
Western Rd. PO6: Cosh 3G 29
  (not continuous)
  PO9: Hav 1E 33
  PO16: Fare 2B 26
Western Ter. PO2: Ports 3G 41
Western Way PO12: Gos 4A 48
  PO16: Fare 2A 26
WESTFIELD 4B 54
Westfield Av. PO11: H Isl 4B 54
West Fld. PO2: Ports 3H 25
Westfield Ind. Est. PO8: Horn 6D 6
  PO12: Gos 3C 48
Westfield Oaks PO11: H Isl 4B 54
Westfield Rd. PO4: S'sea 4G 51
  PO6: Cosh 3C 28
  PO12: Gos 2B 48
Westgate PO14: Stub 4E 37
Westgate Leisure
  Bourne 2G 35
West Haye Rd. PO11: H Isl 6F 55
West Hayling Local Nature Reserve 1A 44
WEST HILL PARK 3B 24
Westland Dr. PO7: Purb 5G 19
  PO13: Lee S 2E 47
Westland Gdns. PO12: Gos 4C 48
Westlands Gro. PO16: Portc 4A 28
West La. PO11: H Isl 3A 54
WEST LEIGH 4G 21
West Leigh Pk. 5G 21
Westley Gro. PO16: Fare 3H 25
West Lodge PO13: Lee S 6F 37
Westmead Cl. PO11: H Isl 4H 53

West M. PO17: K Vil 2G 13
Westminster Pl. PO1: Ports 6H 41
WESTON 6A 56
Weston Av. PO4: S'sea 3H 51
Weston Ct. PO1: Ports 3H 5
Weston Ho. GU32: Pet 4C 56
Weston La. GU32: W'ton 6A 56
Weston Rd. GU31: Pet 4E 57
Weston Way PO3: Ports 5D 42
West Point PO13: Lee S 1C 46
Westside Vw. PO7: W'lle 6E 9
West St. PO1: Ports 6A 4 (4H 49)
  PO9: Bed, Hav 1D 32
  PO10: Ems 3D 34
  PO14: Titch 3B 24
  PO16: Fare 2A 26
  (not continuous)
  PO16: Portc 3H 27
  (not continuous)
  PO17: S'wick 3C 16
WEST TOWN 4A 54
West Vw. Cotts. PO10: S'brne 1H 35
Westway PO15: Titch 6A 12
Westways PO9: Bed 3H 31
  PO14: Stub 3F 37
Westwood Ct. PO10: Ems 1E 35
Westwood Rd. PO2: Ports 1A 42
Wetherdown GU31: Pet 4E 57
Weyhill Cl. PO9: Hav 4D 20
Weymouth Av. PO12: Gos 5F 39
Weymouth Rd. PO2: Ports 4H 41
Whaddon Chase PO14: Stub 3D 36
Whaddon Ct. PO9: Hav 3C 20
Whale Island Way PO2: Ports 4G 41
Whaley Rd. PO2: Ports 4F 41
Wharf Rd. PO2: Ports 5G 41
Wheatcroft Rd. PO13: Lee S 1D 46
Wheatear Dr. GU31: Pet 4G 57
Wheatlands Av. PO11: H Isl 6G 55
Wheatlands Cres. PO11: H Isl 6G 55
Wheatley Grn. PO9: Hav 3C 20
Wheatsheaf Dr. PO8: Cowp 4F 9
Wheatsheaf M. PO9: Hav 4D 20
Wheatstone Rd. PO4: S'sea 4G 51
Wheeler Cl. PO12: Gos 1D 48
Wherwell Cl. PO9: Hav 4H 21
Whichers Cl. PO9: R Cas 1H 21
Whichers Ga. Rd. PO9: R Cas 1H 21
Whitehall Apts. PO2: Ports 5H 41
  (off Malthouse Rd.)
Whimbrel Cl. PO4: S'sea 2B 52
Whinchat Cl. PO15: Fare 5E 13
Whippingham Cl. PO6: Cosh 3H 29
Whiston Ho. PO12: Gos 6A 40
Whitcombe Gdns. PO3: Ports 1F 51
Whiteacres PO12: Gos 2D 48
Whitebeam Cl. PO8: Horn 2C 10
  PO14: Fare 3G 25
White Beam Ri. PO8: Clan 2G 7
Whitechimney Row PO10: Westb 6F 23
Whitecliffe Av. PO3: Ports 6C 42
Whitecliffe Ct. PO12: Gos 3H 47
White Cloud Pk. PO4: S'sea 4F 51
White Cloud Pl. PO4: S'sea 4F 51
Whitecross Gdns. PO2: Ports 2B 42
Whitedell La. PO17: Fare 5D 14
White Dirt La. PO8: Cath 3B 6
White Hart All. 6B 4 (4A 50)
White Hart Cotts. GU31: Pet 4D 56
White Hart La. PO16: Portc 4H 27
White Hart Rd. PO1: Ports 6B 4 (4A 50)
  PO12: Gos 3D 48
Whitehaven PO8: Horn 1D 10
  PO16: Portc 4H 27
White Horse La. PO7: Den 1C 8
White Ho. Gdns. GU32: Pet 2C 56
White Ladies Cl. PO9: Hav 2G 33
Whiteland Way PO8: Clan 2H 7
WHITELEY 1A 12
WHITELEY FARM RDBT. 1A 12
Whiteley La. PO15: Titch 6B 12
  PO15: White 1A 12
Whiteley Shop. Cen. 1A 12
Whiteley Way PO15: White 1A 12
White Lion Wlk. PO12: Gos 2F 49
White Lodge Gdns. PO16: Fare 5G 13
White Oak Wlk. PO9: Hav 4H 21
Whites Ct. PO2: Ports 4H 41
Whites Pl. PO12: Gos 2D 48
White Swan Rd. PO1: Ports 3E 5 (2B 50)
Whitethorn Rd. PO11: H Isl 4D 54

White Wings Ho. PO7: Den 4B 8
Whiting Ho. PO16: Fare 2B 26
Whitley Cl. PO10: Westb 4F 23
Whitley Row PO4: S'sea 2A 52
Whitsbury Rd. PO9: Hav 4G 21
Whitstable Rd. PO6: Cosh 3A 30
Whittington Ct. PO10: Ems 3D 34
Whittington Rd. GU31: Pet 6C 56
Whitwell Rd. PO4: S'sea 6E 51
Whitworth Cl. PO12: Gos 3D 48
Whitworth Rd. PO2: Ports 5B 42
  PO12: Gos 3C 48
Whyke Cl. PO9: Hav 1E 33
WICKHAM 1A 14
Wickham Ct. PO12: Gos 4H 47
Wickham Cft. PO17: Wick 2A 14
Wickham Rd. PO16: Fare 5B 14
  PO17: Fare 3B 14
Wickham St. PO1: Ports 2B 4 (2A 50)
Wickor Cl. PO10: Ems 1E 35
Wickor Way PO10: Ems 6E 23
Wicor Mill La. PO16: Portc 4H 27
Wicor Path PO16: Portc 5B 28
  (Bayly Av.)
  PO16: Portc 4G 27
  (Heritage Gdns.)
Widgeon Cl. PO12: Gos 6H 39
Widgeon Ct. PO16: Portc 3F 27
WIDLEY 1E 31
Widley Ct. PO14: Fare 5A 26
Widley Ct. Dr. PO6: Cosh 4C 30
Widley Gdns. PO7: Wid 6F 19
Widley Rd. PO2: Ports 3G 41
  PO6: Cosh 3C 30
Widley Wlk. PO7: Purb 1B 30
Wield Cl. PO9: Hav 5C 20
Wigan Cres. PO9: Bed 1B 32
Wight Vw. PO13: Lee S 6F 37
Wigmore Ho. PO1: Ports 1D 50
Wilberforce Rd. PO5: S'sea 6F 5 (4C 50)
  PO12: Gos 6E 49
Wilby La. PO3: Ports 1E 43
Wild Flower Dr. PO15: Titch 6A 12
Wild Grounds Nature Reserve 6B 38
Wildmoor Wlk. PO9: Hav 4H 21
Wild Ridings PO14: Fare 3D 24
Wilkins Cl. PO8: Clan 1F 7
Willersley Cl. PO6: Cosh 2G 29
William Booth Ho. PO1: Ports 1D 4 (2B 50)
William Cl. PO14: Stub 4F 37
William Ct. PO3: Ports 1G 51
William George Ct. PO13: Lee S 2C 46
William Price Gdns. PO16: Fare 1B 26
Williams Cl. PO13: Gos 6D 38
Williams Rd. PO3: Ports 2D 42
William Tite Ct. PO12: Gos 1B 48
Willis Rd. PO1: Ports 2F 5 (2C 50)
  PO12: Gos 3E 49
  (not continuous)
Willis Ter. GU32: Pet 4C 56
Willow Cl. PO9: Hav 2G 33
Willow Ct. PO16: Fare 2G 25
Willowdene Cl. PO9: Bed 5B 20
Willow Dr. GU31: Pet 6D 56
Willow Gdns. PO10: Westb 5F 23
Willow Pl. PO12: Gos 2D 48
The Willows PO2: Ports 3G 41
  PO7: Den 3A 8
Willowside PO8: Cowp 2H 9
Willow Tree Av. PO8: Cowp 5B 10
Willow Tree Gdns. PO14: Fare 3G 25
Willow Wood Rd. PO11: H Isl 4C 54
Wilmcote Gdns. PO5: S'sea 5D 50
Wilmcote Ho. PO5: S'sea 4H 5 (2D 50)
Wilmott Cl. PO12: Gos 2B 48
Wilmott La. PO12: Gos 2B 48
Wilson Gro. PO5: S'sea 4D 50
Wilson Rd. PO2: Ports 3G 41
Wilton Cl. PO12: Gos 3B 48
Wilton Dr. PO8: Horn 2A 10
Wilton Exchange PO5: S'sea 6G 5
Wilton Pl. PO5: S'sea 5D 50
Wilton Ter. PO5: S'sea 5D 50
Wiltshire Sq. PO5: Seg 6B 12
Wiltshire St. PO5: S'sea 4E 5 (3B 50)
Wilverley Av. PO9: Hav 5G 21
Wimbledon Pk. Rd. PO5: S'sea 5D 50
Wimbledon Pk. Sports Cen. 5D 50
Wimborne Rd. PO4: S'sea 3G 51
Wimpole Ct. PO1: Ports 1E 51
Wimpole St. PO1: Ports 1D 50
Wincanton Way PO7: W'lle 6B 10
Winchcombe Rd. PO6: Cosh 2F 29

GUIDE TO SELECTED PLACES OF INTEREST

HOW TO USE THE GUIDE

Opening times for places of interest vary considerably depending on the season, day of the week or the ownership of the property. Please check opening times before starting your journey.

The index reference is to the square in which the place of interest appears. e.g. **City Museum** 6D **4**, is to be found in square 6D on page 4.

PORTSMOUTH

Portsmouth is an important naval port, ferry port, historic city and, together with Southsea, a family holiday resort.

With its superb natural harbour the dockyard has been a naval base since the 13th century, (see below). The Royal Dockyard became an immense industrial complex driving the growth in both the size and prosperity of the city.

Both Charles Dickens and Isambard Brunel were born here. The seaside resort of Southsea boasts four miles of beach and seafront facilities, while Portsmouth is all things pertaining to the sea, with its activities, water sports and boat trips.

Visitor Information Centres

The Hard, **Portsmouth**, PO1 3PA.   3B **4**

Museum Road, **Portsmouth**, P01 2LJ.   5D **4**
Tel: 023 9282 6722

South Street, **Gosport**, PO12 1EP.   3G **49**
Tel: 023 9252 2944

Central Beachlands,   5A **54**
Hayling Island, PO11 0AG.
Tel: 023 9246 7111

For information on accommodation, transport, tours of the harbour, maps, guidebooks and souvenirs.

www.visitportsmouth.co.uk

Harbour Tours

Portsmouth Harbour Tour, Tel: 01983 564602
www.portsmouth-boat-trips.co.uk
45 minute trips around the Harbour, including the Royal Naval Base from either the Historic Dockyard or Gunwharf Quays.

See also: Portsmouth Historic Dockyard.

© Bruce Turner. image from BigStockPhoto.com

HMS Warrior 1860

Portsmouth Harbour

© Pawel Nawrot. image from BigStockPhoto.com

Portsmouth Historic Dockyard Visitor Centre, Victory Gate PO1 3LJ
Tel: 023 9283 9766
www.historicdockyard.co.uk or for more background information www.portsmouthdockyard.org.uk

The founding of the Royal Dockyard in 1212 was at the command of King John, although it didn't flourish until Edward II made it the headquarters of the southern division of the navy. The building of the first dry-dock in 1495, ordered by Henry VII, and of the Mary Rose in 1509, the flagship of Henry VIII's Royal Navy, further increased the importance of Portsmouth.

Throughout the 17th and 18th centuries the dockyard was enlarged with some of today's familiar buildings, including those that house the National Museum of the Royal Navy Portsmouth. As the focus of naval operations moved to the Atlantic Ocean and steam ships replaced sailing ships, Portsmouth, along with Plymouth, gradually replaced Chatham as the Royal Navy's main base of operations. Although still an active military base, the Historic Dockyard has some of the country's most iconic tourist naval attractions.

HMS Victory

Harbour Tour — 2A 4

A 45 minute tour of the harbour is included as part of the Historic Dockyard 'All Attraction Ticket'. Boats depart from the jetty near HMS Warrior 1860.

HMS M.33 — 1A 4

This warship, in its distinctive black and white dazzle paint, is a survivor of the First World War Gallipoli Campaign. Sitting in a dry dock, visitors can explore where the 72 men on board lived and fought. There is access to the Captain's quarters, galley, wheelhouse and the upper decks where two 6" guns will impress. The horror and destruction of the Gallipoli Campaign, and the role the ship and crew took in it, is conveyed in a 10 minute film.

HMS Victory — 1A 4

Tel: 023 9283 9766. www.hms-victory.com
Nelson's Battle of Trafalgar flagship is arguably the Royal Navy's most famous warship. Led by historical and archaelogical research, Victory has been painted in her Battle of Trafalgar colours to present her in a more authentic way as part of an ongoing conservation programme. The visitor experience onboard is brought alive with hand held audio guides with accounts from a cast of nine characters as HMS Victory sets sail for the battle of Trafalgar. With increased access to areas of the ship, the scene is set for visitors to follow in the footsteps of Nelson and his crew. A brass plaque marks the spot on the quarter deck where Nelson fell, shot at the height of the battle in 1805.

Action Stations — 2B 4

Tel: 023 9289 3338. www.actionstations.org
Housed in Boathouse 6, this visitor attraction combines physical activity and interactive fun to demonstrate the challenges and excitement of life in the modern Royal Navy. Scale the 28ft (8.4m) Climbing Tower against the clock, attack the Ninja Force assault course, test yourself by playing computer games in the Ops Room and take a white-knuckle ride in the motion simulator.

HMS Warrior 1860 — 3A 4

Tel: 023 9277 8600. www.hmswarrior.org
Built in 1860, this was Britain's first iron-hulled warship. Powered by both steam and sail she was the largest, fastest and most fearsome naval weapon of her day. Step on board to explore her four vast decks and enter the world of a Victorian sailor.

Mary Rose Museum   1A 4

Tel: 023 9281 2931. www.maryrose.org
The Tudor war ship Mary Rose was famously raised in 1982 under the gaze of a worldwide television audience. A favourite ship of Henry VIII she sank accidentally during an engagement with the French fleet in 1545. Buried in the The Solent mud, one complete side was preserved together with many thousands of personal and military artifacts that have greatly enlarged knowledge of 16th century maritime life and warfare. The boat-shaped museum has displays of these beautifully preserved Tudor artefacts, and shows the history of the ship and the Tudor navy.

National Museum of the Royal Navy   2A 4
Portsmouth

Tel: 023 9283 9766.
www.nmrn-portsmouth.org.uk
The museum is principally housed in three former dockyard buildings and tells the story of the Royal Navy and its importance in shaping the history of Britain. 'HMS - Hear My Story' is a major exhibition that brings you closer to the real Navy, telling the stories of the ordinary men, women and ships, both in war and during peacetime. The 'Sailing Navy Gallery' offers a revised view of life aboard the great sailing warships; its interactive and hands-on approach will engage visitors of all ages and abilities. Nelson, the man, his life and career can be better understood in the 'Nelson Gallery' which includes some of his personal belongings. The 'Victory Gallery' complements a visit to HMS Victory, telling the story of the famous ship from the laying of her keel in 1759 to present day preservation. The immersive visitor experience 'Trafalgar!' puts you in the middle of the action on a gun deck during the battle. By contrast, walk among the beautifully carved, late 18th century, ship figureheads in the 'Spirit of the Figurehead' display. The fore topsail from HMS Victory, the 'Trafalgar Sail', is on display; shot through some 90 times this battle-scarred sail, the ship's second largest, is testament to the ferocity of the Battle of Trafalgar. There is also a changing programme of special exhibitions; currently for 2017, 'Women and the Royal Navy' - check the web site for the latest information.

Aboard HMS Victory

SELECTED PLACES OF INTEREST

Blue Reef Aquarium   6C 50

Clarence Esplanade, Southsea PO5 3PB.
Tel: 023 9287 5222.
www.bluereefaquarium.co.uk/portsmouth
Discover the amazing world under the sea at this award winning aquarium. Encounter both local and tropical species of aquatic life; walk through the underwater tunnel in the giant ocean tank and enjoy informative talks and feeding sessions.

Charles Dickens Birthplace Museum   6G 41

393 Old Commercial Road PO1 4QL.
Tel: 023 9282 7261.
www.charlesdickensbirthplace.co.uk
Charles Dickens was born here in 1812. Three principal rooms are fully furnished in the style of the period, together with memorabilia and an exhibition display featuring both Dickens and the City of Portsmouth.

Cumberland House Natural History Museum   6F **51**

Eastern Parade PO4 9RF. Tel: 023 9281 5276.
www.portsmouthnaturalhistory.co.uk
The Museum displays selected items from a diverse collection of over 114,000 natural science specimens. In addition, a brand-new Butterfly House is planned and the recent introduction of an observational beehive is proving to be of particular interest.

D-Day Museum & Overlord Embroidery   6C **50**

Clarence Esplanade, Southsea PO5 3NT.
Tel: 023 9282 6772.
www.ddaymuseum.co.uk
Currently being refurbished; reopens in 2018.
Galleries tell the story of the 1944 Normandy landings using objects and interactive material along with first-hand documented accounts - from the planning and build up, to the actual day. Its centrepiece is the Overlord Embroidery, a 34 panel Bayeux Tapestry inspired work.

Diving Museum   5H **47**

No 2 Battery, Stokes Bay Road, Gosport PO12 2QU.
www.divingmuseum.co.uk
Housed in a former coastal defence gun battery, the museum exhibits the best range of military, commercial and recreational diving equipment in Europe.

Explosion! Museum of Naval Firepower   6B **40**

Heritage Way, Priddy's Hard,
Gosport PO12 4LE.
Tel: 023 9250 5600.
www.explosion.org.uk
This award winning museum occupies 18th century buildings centred on the original powder magazine. The museum tells the story of munitions workers over the centuries and includes an extensive collection of small arms, shells, torpedoes and modern missiles.

© Dave Timms. image from BigStockPhoto.com

Portchester Castle Moat

Fort Brockhurst   4F **39**

Gunner's Way,
Gosport PO12 4DS.
Tel: 02392 581059.
www.english-heritage.org.uk/visit/places/fort-brockhurst
Built as part of the extensive defence network around Portsmouth in the mid 19th century this massive moated fort is also used by English Heritage as a store for reserve collections of historic artifacts.

Fort Nelson (Royal Armouries Museum)   6H **15**

Portsdown Hill Road,
Fareham PO17 6AN.
Tel: 013 2923 3734.
www.royalarmouries.org/visit-us/fort-nelson
Fort Nelson is home to the Royal Armouries collection of artillery. Its extensive holdings cover armaments from all periods and countries, while imaginative and informative set displays trace the history, theory and practice of firepower, demonstrated every day with the live firing of one of the Museum's field guns. Fort Nelson is a historic artillery emplacement, built in the 1860s and set in a commanding position on Portsdown Hill with panoramic views over Portsmouth Harbour and Spithead.

Gunwharf Quays   4B **4**

Gunwharf Quays PO1 3TZ.
Tel: 023 9283 6700.
www.gunwharf-quays.com
As well as nearly 100 shops and over 30 restaurants and bars, there is a cinema, night club, art gallery, casino, fitness centre and 10-pin bowling centre, all under one roof.

'Onboard' Charters   4A **4**

Gunwharf Quays PO1 3TZ.
Tel: 023 9200 6427.
www.onboardcharters.com
Experience the thrill of high speed RIB powerboats or luxury power-cruisers. Trips of different duration are available, including: the Mary Rose wreck site; exploring the Harbour and out to the Solent Forts.

Portchester Castle   5D **28**

Church Road, Portchester PO16 9QW.
www.english-heritage.org.uk/visit/places/portchester-castle
An impressive late 3rd century Roman fort with Norman keep and other later additions constructed to defend the northern edge of Portsmouth Harbour. The massive 100 ft keep formed part of a 14th century Royal Palace built for Richard II. Although the floor and roof structures have long since gone, the window

openings and beam sockets make it easy to understand the once regal apartments.

Portsmouth Museum 6D 4

Museum Road PO1 2LJ. Tel: 023 9283 4779.
www.portsmouthcitymuseums.co.uk
Devoted to the history of Portsmouth and its inhabitants, the collections illustrate how the city has grown and life styles have changed as a result. There is also a fine and decorative arts gallery with a changing mixture of works on display.

Port Solent 4E 29

Port Solent PO6 4TP.
Tel: 023 9221 0606.
www.portsolent.com
There are shops, restaurants, a cinema and fitness centre, as well numerous special events held at this modern development alongside an attractive marina.

Portsmouth Cathedral 6B 4

High Street PO1 2HH.
Tel: 023 9282 3300.
www.portsmouthcathedral.org.uk
A 12th century medieval church with central 17th century tower. Its colourful history includes coming under attack by French raiders in 1337 and by Parliamentary forces during the Civil War. Adopted as Cathedral for Portsmouth in 1927 and subsequently enlarged to suit this new role.

Royal Navy Submarine Museum 4G 49

Haslar Jetty Road,
Gosport PO12 2AS.
Tel: 023 9251 0354.
www.submarine-museum.co.uk
Discover the history of the submarine, the life of submariners and underwater warfare. Visitors can take a tour of HMS Alliance, a diesel electric submarine built in 1945, the only remaining example from the Second World War. Other submarines of note include the Holland 1, Britain's first Royal Navy submarine built in 1901, on display in a climate controlled building and the X24 midget submarine. In addition the museum also contains thousands of photographs, documents and artefacts.

Round Tower 6A 4

Broad Street PO1 2JE
www.portsmouthmuseums.co.uk/museum-service/The-Round-Tower
Together with the Square Tower, the Round Tower formed part of the 15th century defence of The Point, the entrance to Portsmouth Harbour. Today, great sea

and city views can be taken from the top of the tower and local artists can be visited to see their work in the renovated arches of Hotwalls Studios.

Royal Garrison Church 6C 4

Penny Street PO1 2NJ.
www.english-heritage.org.uk/visit/places/royal-garrison-church-portsmouth
Originally built in the 13th century, the church was part of a hospital and pilgrim hostel. After the reformation the building was used to house ammunition, then part of the Governor of Portsmouth's house during Elizabeth I's reign, before becoming the church for the forces in the 1580s. Restored in the 19th century and badly damaged in a 1941 firebomb raid, the church has fine stained-glass windows depicting scenes from its own history.

© Nick Hawkes. image from BigStockPhoto.com

Royal Garrison Church

Royal Marines Museum

www.royalmarinesmuseum.co.uk
The Museum's galleries are now closed in Eastney Esplanade, although the building will remain as a venue until the end of 2018. The SeaMore project will see the museum move to new galleries, opening in 2020, within Portsmouth Historic Dockyard.

Southsea Castle 6C 50

Clarence Esplanade PO5 3PA.
Tel: 023 9282 6722.
www.southseacastle.co.uk
The Castle was built in 1544, part of the important Tudor defence fortifications along the coast. It was from here, a year later, that Henry VIII watched the Mary Rose capsize while engaging French galleys. A long history of military service ended here in 1960 when the castle was sold to Portsmouth City Council. Visitors can explore the keep, enter a 19th century tunnel built to defend the moat, and appreciate the fabulous views across the Solent from the castle ramparts.

Stefan Muran. image from BigStockPhoto.com

Spinnaker Tower, Gunwharf Quays

Spinnaker Tower   4A 4

Gunwharf Quays PO1 3TT.
Tel: 023 9285 7520.
www.spinnakertower.co.uk
This dramatic 170 metre high landmark and observation tower provides 360° views over Portsmouth and the south coast. Discover the stories behind the view and visit the Sky Deck, which is open to the elements, or dare to cross the glass floor of the Sky Walk! Thrillseekers can book selected dates between April and September to abseil 100 metres down the side of the iconic structure.

Square Tower   6A 4

Broad Street PO1 2JE.
www.portsmouthmuseums.co.uk/museum-service/
The-Square-Tower and www.squaretower.co.uk
The establishment of a navy dockyard by Henry VII prompted the strengthening of harbour defences, work that included the building of the Square Tower. The massive stone structure has been a gunpowder store, Governor's House and meat store; today it is mainly an events venue.

Titchfield Abbey   1C 24

Mill Lane, Fareham PO15 5RA.
Tel: 037 0333 1181.
www.english-heritage.org.uk/visit/places/
titchfield-abbey
A ruined 13th century abbey. The abbey church was converted, in Tudor times, into an imposing castellated gatehouse mansion by the 1st Earl of Southampton following the dissolution of the monasteries by Henry VIII. Henry was among the several notable visitors to be later entertained here.

SAFETY CAMERA INFORMATION

PocketGPSWorld.com's CamerAlert is a self-contained speed and red light camera warning system for SatNavs and Android or Apple iOS smartphones/tablets. Visit www.cameralert.com to download.

Safety camera locations are publicised by the Safer Roads Partnership which operates them in order to encourage drivers to comply with speed limits at these sites. It is the driver's absolute responsibility to be aware of and to adhere to speed limits at all times.

By showing this safety camera information it is the intention of Geographers' A-Z Map Company Ltd., to encourage safe driving and greater awareness of speed limits and vehicle speed. Data accurate at time of printing.